Creating Your Soul Map:

Manifesting the Future You with a Vision Board

By

Jeremy Lopez

Creating Your Soul Map:

Manifesting the Future You with a Vision Board

Copyright © 2018 Dr. Jeremy Lopez

Published by Identity Network

P.O. Box 383213

Birmingham, AL, 35238

CONTENTS

ENDORSEMENTS

"This fast-moving and enjoyable book is loaded with insights and ideas to help you achieve all your goals – faster than ever before." – Greg S. Reid, *Forbes* and *Inc.* top-rated Keynote Speaker

"You are put on this earth with incredible potential and a divine destiny. This powerful, practical man shows you how to tap into powers you didn't even know you had." – Brian Tracy – Author, *The Power of Self Confidence*

"Jeremy has drawn from the wells of his prophetic anointing very insightful revelation for us today, securing the reader in a fortress of truth." – Roberts Liardon

"It is a transformational book that challenges you to rethink what you have been taught while reflecting more deeply upon the truth you have come to know. The journey through this book is prophetic, mystical, and magical." – Robert Ricciardelli – Founder – *The Converging Zone Network*

PREFACE

For as long as I can even remember, I have been a student of the things of the Spirit. It was more than three decades ago that I found myself literally consumed by the power of that Spirit, and an insatiable, innate hunger began to develop within me to uncover the deeper and greater mysteries of Creation. Not a single day has gone by, throughout these past three decades of my work, that I have not been reminded of the all-encompassing power of vision and the integral role that visualization plays within the life of each and every individual, here partaking of this earthly experience within the physical plane. My life was forever changed, in an instant, the moment I found myself awakened to the reality that visualization is, in many regards, a driving force of all that we do, all that we say, and all that we think, while we're here. In fact, visualization is hardwired into the Law of Creation and The Law of Attraction so much so that it is literally impossible to exist without the component of vision. We are created by divine design to be visual creatures – powerful spirit beings who have been graced with the ability to *see* the world we now find ourselves enjoying. For years, I have written and spoken about the power of vision, as it relates to The Law of Attraction and the ability we each possess to create the lives we truly desire. Fortunately, now, in this day in time, I see a new hunger within the world as never before, as men and women, young and old, are finally beginning to become awakened to the power of visualization. With popular, best-selling books now available worldwide which detail the power of the Law of Attraction, there is now so much talk about vision boards and dream boards. Although I've utilized a vision board in my own life for decades and have taught many countless others the significance of utilizing this powerful tool within their own lives, very little knowledge seems to exist within the world about just how important vision boards are and even less knowledge seems to be available about how to properly assemble and how to use a vision board. I'm writing this book to you, my dear fellow seeker and student of the Spirit, in order to change that. To my knowledge, this is the very first book of its kind – a book which not only discusses in great detail the importance of a vision board but also delves deeply into the mechanics of how a vision board operates. For years, I've been asked by readers and students throughout the world to discuss openly, both, the science and the spirituality behind the vision board. Now, that time has finally come. I offer this insight to you because I know, from years of vast experience working with the powerful Law of Attraction and the powerful Law of Creation, that what you are able to truly envision, you are truly able to create.

INTRODUCTION

For weeks, each day I've driven by a massive construction project now currently underway in my home city. Only blocks from the offices of Identity Network is emerging the massive steel skeleton of a building under construction. Within the year, new and beautiful luxury condos will be available to buyers. For the time being, though, there is still much work to be done. As I drive past, I so often find myself thinking about the vast amount of work that must go into such a major undertaking – into the process of building, that is. For every beam being raised each day, there is so much more work being enacted behind the scenes. For every movement that onlookers are able to see, there is so much more that is happening just beyond natural sight. However, from the planning to the financing to the clearing to the construction itself, it all began with a vision and with a blueprint. It all began with a mental image – an internal picture – within the mind of the developer. In a very real sense, isn't that always the case, though? If we were to be completely honest with ourselves, wouldn't we be forced to admit that literally every aspect of life experience is directly dependent upon an inner vision and what we choose to see about ourselves? With each and every thought comes an internal, mental picture and image. We are visual beings by design, so artfully and so meticulously crafted by the Creator that we possess the Divine ability to see – both with our natural eyes and also within our own souls. Because of this innate ability to *see* we also possess the ability to envision and to plan. With our inner visions – the internal imagery of the soul – we are given the unique ability to look ahead and to envision ourselves in a future time. Because of the soul, each day we dream and daydream, often imagining ourselves living out the pictures which seem to so randomly fill the screens of our mind. As I've shared on many occasions, particularly in my books *The Universe Is At Your Command* and *Creating With Your Thoughts*, the mind and the spirit and the soul are so deeply and so intrinsically interwoven that in order to truly master the processes behind our own creative power we must begin to see behind our thoughts in order to truly see our deepest and most heart-felt desires. In more than three decades of my work and calling, immersing myself into the magical world of the Spirit and of the Divine

Mind, I've seen, firsthand, how the process of creating and manifesting desire is the result of learning to match the inner vision with the outer vision and to come into alignment with both. You see, each and every building project begins, first, with a blueprint – a visual image that can be looked upon. Without these blueprints, how would the builders – those tasked with completing the work – know how to implement the instructions given? Think of this for a moment. Could you imagine the literal and dangerous mess that would ensue if, when attempting to build a new home, the contractors were never given a blueprint to follow? What would happen if, after deciding to build a home or a hotel or a gigantic skyscraper, the builders were told, simply, "Just do whatever you feel?" Not only would build codes be violated each and every day during the building process but, needless to say, the project would never be completed because there would never be any real agreement. One builder might envision beautiful, marble floors, while another might picture, instead, stained wood. Suffice it to say, the building project would fall into absolute disarray almost immediately. However, as outlandish as that scenario might seem, did you know that for years and years that is exactly what you've allowed to happen in your own, daily life if you haven't maintained some vision for your outcome? It's true. Just as in the natural, physical world, disaster and catastrophe ensues when blueprints are not followed, the same can be said of the spiritual world when speaking of The Law of Attraction. In truth, one needs to look no further than the Hindenburg disaster or the Titanic to see that things do not always go according to plan, even with a blueprint. Imagine attempting to build without one. For decades, when speaking with clients who have come to me for life coaching sessions, one of the very first questions I've asked them is, "Do you have a vision board?" More times than not, often by just listening to the stories of their experiences, I already know the answer. Usually the answer is "No." Sometimes, though, the answer is "What's that?" Well, let's start from the very beginning, shall we? If we're going to delve deeply into the mechanics behind a vision board, let's start with some basics. What is it? A vision board – sometimes referred to as a dream board – is, quite simply, a tool to aid in the process of visualization. The vision board, itself, is nothing more than that. Vision boards can take on many different and varying forms, really. From notebooks to journals to beautiful, detailed posters to even crumpled pieces of napkin, a vision board is simply a visual aid used to remind us of our desires and intended outcomes. Although the vision board, itself, possesses no power, apart from the intention we place into it with our thoughts, this powerful tool can lead to very real and life-changing results very quickly, as you will soon discover. The reason to have a vision board is really quite simple: "Write it down." Vision boards have actually been around for millennia and have been used by, both, young and old, regardless of background, culture, or creed. One of the most notable examples of the use of a vision board can be found, rather astonishingly in fact, in a passage of scripture within the Holy Bible. In the Book of Habakkuk, we are given a glimpse into the Divine, spiritual power put into practice when one's vision is made plain. "And the LORD answered me and said, *Write the vision, and make it plain upon tables,* that he may run that readeth it. For the *vision* is yet for an appointed time, but at the end it shall speak, and not lie: though it tarry, wait for it; because it will surely come, it will not tarry." (Habakkuk 2:2-3) There is so much more to be said of this passage of scripture, as we will soon discuss; however, in this account described we see two very important principles of visualization at work, as it relates to the concept of manifestation: write it down and make it plain. When speaking of vision boards, we are not speaking of something foreign or mystical. No.

In fact we are speaking of something very practical and very real. However, in studying the usage of vision boards throughout the centuries and in recognizing how vision boards are even now currently being used by heads of companies to promote growth in business and increase in wealth, it has become very clear to me that there is a very real spiritual component at work when one begins to utilize a vision board and the immense benefits of this spiritual power at work simply cannot be understated. So much of what the world today now recognizes as Identity Network – the global outreach of my prophetic, empowerment work – began, quite literally, with a vision board. In fact, now, more than three decades later, I still have within my office some of my very first vision boards I created when I was just beginning my work within the prophetic. These are reminders to me of not only the faithfulness of the Spirit but they also serve as a powerful testament to the universal power of The Law of Attraction and The Law of Creation. As I shared in my book, *Creating With Your Thoughts*, we, as individuals, have been endued with all power to manifest the lives we truly desire. In fact, the very power which framed the universe and formed the worlds now in existence is the same power which now resides within us and which is continually being enacted by our own thoughts. It really is true. "If you want to change your life, change your thoughts." I so often share my own, personal mantra with clients in my coaching sessions and say, "I am a firm believer in thinking it, believing it, and then having it! If you can think it, then you can have it!" When I began my work within the prophetic arts all those years ago and began life coaching, there was no talk whatsoever about vision boards and the importance of visualization. In fact, when I spoke to clients about the importance of writing down their visions, so often they looked at me with a look of bewilderment as if I was crazy! Very little was said in those days about The

Law of Attraction and The Law of Creation, particularly within the charismatic circles of Christianity at that time. Religion, it seemed, always had a way of arousing excitement within us about the future promises of God, yet never shared with us the role we were to play in bringing about the manifestations we desired. We were told, quite simply, "Wait on God." However, as I began to study the principles contained within the scriptures and as I researched the science behind visualization and manifestation, recognizing that we are, in fact, hardwired to create what we *see*, I quickly realized the importance of writing down my visions and my dreams. So, some twenty years later, when a very popular, best-selling book titled *The Secret* hit book shelves and heralded the power of The Law of Attraction, I must admit, it really didn't seem like much of a "secret" to me. I'd been practicing visualization for years up to that point and encouraging audiences to do the same. What I did realize, though, was that almost overnight, there seemed to be a newfound interest in vision boards. In fact, like never before, clients were beginning to ask about the importance of writing down their own dreams and their visions and keeping journals. It seemed as though a literal paradigm shift had begun to occur within humanity and a newfound hunger for the things of the Holy

Spirit had been ignited. It was a beautiful thing. Other popular books began to be released and flood the market of the self-help industry – books that continued to herald the importance of visualization and the science behind the power of the mind and Spirit. However, in each book, it seemed as though one element was continually being glossed over and rarely even spoken of: vision boards. I mean, there would be an occasional, honorary mention, at times. There would be a few passages in a book about how important it is to write down your vision or to keep a blueprint of your dreams; however, there was very little detail. When more than twenty clients asked if I would consider writing a book about the power behind vision boards, I took it as confirmation that, perhaps, the world needs this knowledge, in some way. Right now, within a drawer in my desk in my study, there is a folded piece of paper, now worn and yellowed with age. The edges are tattered and there is a slight tear on one side. The date, inscribed at the top, is now a date more than twenty-five years passed. In messy, almost illegible handwriting, I scribbled the following message to the universe: "Within two years, I will have a ministry that reaches the world. I will be an author. I will have my own business. I will own my dream home, debt-free." At the time, there was no beautiful company letterhead to write the message upon. In fact, there was no company and, at the time, I could barely even afford postage. I had written the message to the universe one night, after a time of prayer, after studying the Book of Habakkuk. I wanted to put the principle to the test. At the time, all I knew was that I had a hunger for the things of the Spirit and a message which I wanted the world to hear. Getting a single speaking engagement in those days seemed almost impossible. Not even the local church congregation of eight people seemed to be interested in my prophetic ministry. The idea of speaking to millions of people around the world seemed not only impossible but, in all honesty, it seemed so outlandish and unattainable that even to write down such a dream was a waste of my time. I had nothing, except the power of the Spirit and a vision – and a pen and paper. I had no staff to write the message for me. I had no publishing contract. No media appearances scheduled. As I wrote the message, with tears streaming down my face, it all seemed so futile, at first. Would this even do anything? Really? What, if anything at all, would this change? I took the piece of paper – the message – and set it upon my nightstand beside my bed. The following morning, it was the first thing I saw when I opened my eyes. That night, it was the last thing I gazed upon, as I closed my eyes and drifted to sleep. In case you now find yourself asking if it worked, let me explain the answer to that question. I now wake up each morning in my dream home – which I own – in one of the most beautiful and affluent neighborhoods in my city. I drive to the headquarters of Identity Network and am greeted by a staff I absolutely love and adore. My books are, even as you read this, being read on seven continents throughout the world. I have so many invitations to speak and to minister at churches that I literally have to sometimes decline speaking engagements because it's just impossible to travel to them all. I have an eight month waiting list for clients because of the demand. In short, yes it worked.

It worked beyond even my own wildest dreams. Within months of writing that message to the universe and making the vision plain, I was offered a publishing contract by one of the world's largest publishing companies. Literally, overnight, I became a household name within the prophetic community around the world, when it happened. So, what exactly changed? What exactly happened? Did the vision manifest simply because of my faithfulness and dedication or was something else – something even more supernatural and even more mystical – at work behind the scenes. While so many – even other prophets – were instructing me to simply wait and sit idly by for the Spirit to move, what could have possibly changed to enact the powerful energies of creation within my life so, so very quickly? I mean, really? Well, that, my friend is the inspiration for this book. I had prayed for years and for years had been passionate for the things of the Spirit. I had been faithful in my giving and in my dedication. So, what happened that changed the paradigm of my life? What exactly was it that took the inner vision – my own passionate dreams for a better more fulfilling life – and made it an outward manifestation? What took the inner dream and made it an outward reality, manifested in the physical world for all to see? What was it that transformed the vision within my mind's eye into a very real, physical and tangible reality that I can see with my natural eyes and touch with my natural hand? In short, I wrote it down and I made it plain. A vision board, my friend, is a tool by which we begin to bring into the natural world the dreams, the desires, and the visions of the inner dreamer. It is the catalyst – the threshold – by which the inner is first enacted outwardly. It's a point at which spirit begins to become flesh. Does a vision board work? My friend you have no idea. In this book, we're going to go even deeper, though. Deeper, still, into the hidden recesses of the mind and of the Spirit in order to begin to unlock the true power of creation which begins to be enacted the moment the pen first touches paper – when a vision board is created. Today, my vision boards are much, much more detailed and much, much more presentable. Gone are the days of writing my visions upon pieces of crumpled paper – though I do occasionally write down my ideas for future books upon napkins as I sit in the local coffee shop. Today, my vision boards are much more expansive. Much larger, in content and in actuality. I have different dreams now. I have different visions, with different time tables. I have new things to accomplish and new visions to manifest in my life. So, I continue to write. I continue to create vision boards. I continue to manifest. My friend, I offer you the teachings within this book not only as a testament to what the vision board has meant to my life but, even more so, as a testament to the power of the creative Spirit which we have all been entrusted with by the Creator. You are reading these words now because the inner Creator within you has been awakened. Like never before, you are now beginning to feel the pull of creations' call within your heart. You have visions for your own life, do you not? The new home, the new car, and the new business all exists already, simply waiting to be brought forth into the natural world for you. The new levels of joy, hope, and peace – all of the fruit of the Spirit –

are simply waiting to be harnessed and enacted. What if I were to promise you that within six months you will begin to see very real and visible results within your life if you were to put into practice the principles contained within this book? Would you find that impossible and difficult to believe? If so, then I encourage you to read on. If you are not living the life you truly desire, then that, in itself, is proof-positive that what you've been doing hasn't worked. Why not try to begin to build a new life? All that is needed, first, is a blueprint.

ASPECTS OF DESIRE

ೞೞ

"People don't attract what they think as much as they attract what they truly desire inside their heart." – Jeremy Lopez

False humility is one of the greatest lies of religious indoctrination. I'm absolutely certain of it. By false humility, I mean the religiously programmed response which says, "I don't deserve it." "I'm not good enough." "I can't have it." In order to access the deeper

1

truths of the power of the Spirit and of the Divine Mind, it is imperative to, first, have a proper working knowledge of The Law of Creation. Thoughts become things, as I described extensively in my books *The Universe Is At Your Command* and *Creating With your Thoughts*. We are powerful spirits having a human experience, not depraved, sinful humans here attempting to reconnect with a God of judgment. Jesus settled the issue once for all. Thankfully. So, if you are going to move deeper into the realm of the Spirit and, even more so, into the truth of your own creative power, then you must leave religious nonsense at the door, in order to proceed further. In order to proceed further, we must, first, establish that your desires exist for a very real reason and that you, as a creator in this earth realm, are designed to think and to feel and to experience and that all these experiences here serve as a universal gauge, of sorts, by which you and I can determine – within our minds – the lives that we truly desire. So, beginning right now, I need to make it perfect clear, if we are to proceed further, that I am in no way concerned with what you feel you deserve or do not deserve. If you feel undeserving and see yourself as nothing more than a wretched sinner saved by grace, then I pray that you take that issue up with the Creator, get in touch with your true Self, get a vision for your life which causes you to see yourself the way the Spirit sees you, then come back. If you can, now, see yourself as a powerful, thinking, creative spirit, then let's proceed. As I said, I'm not concerned with what you feel you deserve; I'm concerned with what you truly desire. In other words, what is it that you truly want? Part of the reason that false humility is such a damnable poison of religion is that is causes us to become separated within our minds from the truth that we have unlimited abundance connected to us at all times. Truly, He – the Creator – is in all and through all. You and I are one with all of the abundance of creation. I share much more of this powerful principle of Oneness in my teaching, *Connecting to Creation Resources*, available through Identity Network. If you find yourself reading these words, thinking to yourself, "I *shouldn't* want what I want," then I lovingly encourage you to reference the chapter, entitled "Behind The Thought," in my book *Creating With Your Thoughts*. You might find yourself asking, "Why all the disclaimers?" Well, I promise you there's a reason for it. If you are not absolutely and one-hundred percent ready to begin to manifest your desires, you do not need to proceed with this book. I offer you that disclaimer as a warning, as the teachings contained within this book will absolutely, one-hundred percent cause you to manifest your desires in your life. I want you to be prepared to accept responsibility for what you create. That's how powerful the truths contained within this book are. These principles will absolutely work within your life to manifest your desires and you will see the principles working even before you finish reading the book, so, again, please proceed with caution if you are not absolutely ready to change your life and get exactly what you want. We're proceeding, together, on this spiritual journey, with the understanding that you are a conscientious, responsible creator who is well aware of the power of the mind and of the Spirit. I was coaching a young man once, years ago, who had come to me to learn the power of visualization. I offered him the same warning I just offered you, the reader. I still remember him so vividly, to this very day. On his way to work one morning, while commuting on the subway in his city, he stepped onto the train, just like every other morning – coffee and a newspaper in hand – when he first saw her. She was seated, alone. He had taken the train every morning and had never seen her before. He instantly felt a sort of magnetic draw to her. But he didn't speak. "I regretted it," he later informed me. "I haven't seen her since. I should have approached her and attempted to speak to her." When he first came to me, he explained, "I can't stop thinking about her. I'd give anything to have another chance to speak with her." He informed me that he had prayed and prayed, to no avail. Time passed. When I told him the secret of a vision board during one of our coaching sessions, I gave it very little thought, at the time. Six months later he reached out to me to describe how, only five days after implementing a vision board into his practice of prayer, visualization and meditation, he took the train for the morning commute and saw her again. He went on to explain that she approached him and asked if she could have his number. "She wouldn't stop calling," he said. "It was really overwhelming. I couldn't even finish my work at the office because I would continuously be interrupted with text messages throughout the day." Now, do you see why I offer you the warning and encouraged you to proceed with caution? The moment that you and I come into alignment with our desire, we will, without question, bring our desire into the physical world every, single time. This is why it is absolutely paramount and critical that you and I be in touch with our true desires because, when we bring those desires into the physical world through the use of a vision board we will have to be prepared to live with the results. Thankfully, he's now happily married – to another woman – and is the proud father of two young daughters. You see, he manifested a desire that he wasn't truly in touch with and it ended up causing him major confusion. That's how powerful desire is, when we learn to harness it and bring it into the natural, three-dimensional world. It will manifest, without question, when we learn to recognize the correlation between our desires and our visualizations, so we should always go deep within ourselves – into the recesses of our own intentions – in order to be absolutely sure that we truly are wanting and desiring what we claim. The Law of Attraction and The Law of Creation, when intermixed with visualization and harnessed intent is a like a literal powder keg of creative power, and desire is the match which lights the fuse. Be careful. Take time now to fully begin to envision the life you truly want for yourself. Weigh the options. Never, under any circumstance, create haphazardly or flippantly. Decide what you truly want – what it is that you really desire – and then make peace with that image, internally. Desire is such an important component of manifesting that it is literally impossible to speak of The Law of Attraction without also speaking of desire. It is important to note: "What you behold, you become." As the internal imagery within begins to flash upon the screen of the mind's eye, what desire feels good? What desire do you wish to proceed with? What would you truly wish to bring forth into the natural world of the earth realm? I often like to consider all of my passing desires as the "rough drafts," if you will, of the building process of creation. I learned years ago that, contrary to what many popular spiritual teachers now seem to suggest, it isn't the thought itself that creates, but it is, rather, the thought placed into alignment with my deepest desire which creates. You see, this is the reason why it is so vitally important to come into alignment with your true desire, long before ever even attempting to put pen to paper and create a vision board. In other words, suffice it to say, the blueprint – the draft – must exist first within the mind of the architect. As powerful creators, you and I are always, at all times, creating drafts of blueprints all throughout the day – blueprints which will serve as the basis of our building projects as we create our daily life experiences, based upon our thoughts. There are many things that I may have desired in the moment, only to realize that the desire soon passed. I'm sure, if you were to be totally honest, you would say the same about your own life experience. Decide what it is that you truly desire. The Law of Creation is such a powerful force that it *will* create both the good and the bad, according to the decrees of your mind, so that's why it's so important that you come to grips with what you truly want. For most of your life, you've perhaps, been a careless creator. For much of your life you've been building without a blueprint – without a centralized vision. You might ask, "Jeremy, how can you say that?" Well, if you now find yourself living a life that is completely devoid of contentment and fulfillment, which feels so very draining and without reward, such a life is, in fact, proof-positive that you have been building without a blueprint. I say this not to condemn or to cast judgment but, rather to point out that all of the life that you now see is the direct result of an entire life of building.

Whether you realize it or not, you've always been building. With each and every thought, each word, and each intention – whether known or unknown – you have been establishing your decrees. Your life is the direct result of your own building. No, a "devil" didn't do it. No, the Lord didn't do it. You did it. You and only you. Personal responsibility can quite often sting and feel uncomfortable, I know; however, it is the building block of creation, I assure you. The moment you awaken and realize that you've always, at all times, been in partnership with the energies of the universe and that you've always, at all times, been responsible for your own life, the sooner you will begin to understand that it is absolutely possible to begin to rebuild again. It's possible to start over and begin anew. Maybe you now find yourself, reading these words, thinking of the life you now find yourself living and maybe you feel the lack of satisfaction and contentment. Perhaps you now find yourself at years and years of life spent so recklessly building without a blueprint – without a focused vision. Well, there's no time quite like the present to begin to rebuild again. The chaos of past builds has, in all actuality, been a blessing in disguise, whether you realize it yet or not. By experiencing a life that you don't want, now, you're able to realize the life you do want. The universe really does work in mysterious ways. Sometimes it takes having to endure what we do not deserve in order to finally see what we do deserve. My friend, you've been deserving of a rewarding life of fulfillment and joy and contentment the entire time, you just never were able to fully realize it. Well, that changed today. Again, I ask you. What do you really want? Truly? Having a clear image in mind of the future you're preparing to build, the final draft of the architect is beginning to be finalized. Soon, it will be time to begin construction.

ASPECTS OF EMOTION

ෆ৪৩

"The strongest thing you have is your heart. If your heart gets ahold of something, it will for sure be yours!" – Jeremy Lopez

When we speak of The Law of Attraction and the process of beginning to build the life you truly desire, it is important to remember that we are speaking of two worlds: the world of the Spirit and the world of flesh. We're speaking of a moment of transition in which that which is within – the internal image – begins to be brought forth into the natural world. There is more to be said about this process and the inner, spiritual, and mystical dynamic of the Spirit within as it relates to the process of creation which you will soon discover, but let us first look at the concept of emotion. I'm sure you're thinking to yourself, "Jeremy, I'm trying to create the life of my dreams, not get in touch with my emotions!" Well, if so, then therein lies the issue, my friend. Emotion and feeling are so intricately interwoven into the fabric of the energy of creation's power that it is literally impossible to not only separate what we create from what we think, but, in turn, it is impossible to separate our creations from our feelings. As we delve into the mystical and supernatural power of creation – which the Creator has entrusted us with – we must first begin to understand that our feelings matter, equally as much as our thoughts do. In fact, the correlation is so real and so tangible that each and every thought is forever linked to the feeling behind it. This is why images conjure emotion within us. Images and ideas trigger certain emotional responses, causing us to either label the feeling as "good" or "bad." When someone says that they are wanting to build the life of their dreams – a life that they truly desire – what they are actually saying, whether they realize it or not, is that they're wanting to create a life that "feels good" to them. Are they not? Sure, when you envision the life you want to manifest for yourself, you might automatically think of the image of the new car, the dream home, the larger bank account, and the supermodel love interest. That's natural. However, whether you realize it or not, those mental images are merely projections of deeper feelings that you'd like to experience and enjoy and bring into your life. This is why it is always so, so very important to begin to look behind the thought and behind the vision in order to get in touch with your truest and deepest intention, prior to beginning to build. Although the image of the dream home may be the internal image that comes to mind, there is a deeper desire for a certain feeling attached to the image. Although the image may be the home, the feeling might be a feeling of contentment or solace or safety. Perhaps you want a home that you can finally own, debt-free and outright. Well, although the internal image may be the home, the feeling behind the image is the feeling of freedom. You want a place to finally call your own. If you want to attract a new love interest into your life, well, the same is true. In fact, this principle of creation is true with literally everything that we want to create!

There is always a feeling and an emotion attached to the image! If you're seeking to attract a new love interest into your life with your vision board, although the image within your mind may very well be someone that you find outrageously attractive, whom you feel so magnetically drawn to, the feeling behind the image is a feeling of love and passion and desire. You see, before we ever even delve into the spiritual mechanics behind a vision board, we must first begin to recognize that what we're truly wanting to attract into our lives is not necessarily the image within our minds as must as it is the feeling associated with those images. Whether you realize it yet, or not, as you will soon see, what you literally want to create when building a better life is a life that *feels* differently. When you say, "I want to create a better life," you're saying to the universe, "I want a life that feels good." So often, when individuals come to me for coaching sessions, I hear so many of them explain how, above everything else, they want to feel a closer connection to God in their lives. When I hear this, I instinctively know that what they're truly wanting for themselves is a life that feels good. The scriptures make it plain that every, single good thing comes from God and that the energy of God is constant and never changes. In truth, not even once have you and I ever been disconnected from God – the Source of Creation – we've simply, at times, *felt* disconnected from our own, creative flow. "Every good gift and every perfect gift is from above, and cometh down from the Father of lights, with whom there is no variableness, neither shadow of turning." (James 1:17) You see, my friend, it's important that we remind ourselves daily of the goodness of creation around us. In truth, there is only one stream of creative power operating in the universe at all times, as you will soon realize. This one, singular stream of energetic power is the force behind all creation. It is the force which spoke the universe into existence, framed the words, and hurled the stars onto the tapestry of the cosmos. This singular energy – which we refer to as God – is always saying "Yes," at all times. So, in truth, it isn't really even a matter of being separated from God, as much as it is that we can so often feel disconnected within our own minds and emotions. When we feel the inner blockages of separation and disconnectedness, we, in turn, begin to feel a sense of lack and hopelessness. If the force of God is *good*, then there are going to be moments when we feel good and then there are going to be moments when we feel not as good. I firmly believe that we should begin to remove the word "bad" from our vocabularies, when speaking of the power of

The Law of Attraction. Like will always attract like. Begin to see, even now, that the life you're experiencing isn't truly *bad*, it's simply not feeling as *good* as you'd like it to feel. I want you to begin to get in touch with your feelings to the point where when you see the images of your desire flash across the screen of your mind's eye that you will be able to automatically sense the feeling associated with those images. With every image comes a feeling, and these feelings are going to play an important role – perhaps even the most important role – when beginning to create your vision board. So, before we even begin to discuss the process of creating a vision board and the powerful, mystical mechanics of the energies behind it, I want you to, right now, begin to learn to associate your images of desire – the car, the boat, the bank account, the home, the business – with feelings. I want you to begin to develop the habit of looking inwardly to the point where with each thought you'll instantly begin to recognize the feeling behind it. This is why I constantly teach that it is so important that we learn to look *behind* the thought in order to see our truest most sincere intention. So, if you found yourself thinking, "Jeremy, just tell us about the vision board," you're now understanding just how important a role emotion and feeling truly play within the process of creation. When I look at the vision boards I've created, which now hang within my office at Identity Network, although my eyes are seeing the words I've written and the images I've pasted onto the board, something else happens within. I feel something. I feel a sense of inspiration. The images trigger the feeling. These feelings – these flashes of inspiration, as I like to call them – are proof-positive that the images upon the board are in alignment with my truest desire. I can remember speaking to a client once who said of her vision board, "It looks like just a board with pictures on it." I responded, "Well, then something is missing." When creating your own vision board for your life, it's so important to come from a place of inspirational feeling. Think of what feels good. Envision the life of your dreams as you create it and learn to recognize that behind the images and behind the words are very real emotions that you want more of. Each thought and each emotion we have is a signal being sent out into the universe. Each thought possesses a certain frequency and a certain vibration, as I discussed in depth in my book, *Creating With Your Thoughts*. It's not only a very real spiritual concept; it's actually very scientific. Albert Einstein, in the 1948 film *Atomic Physics*, said, "It followed from the special theory of relativity that mass and energy are both but different manifestations of the same thing – a somewhat unfamiliar conception for the average mind." In other words, there is one, singular source behind the "thought" and the "thing." That source is the pure energy of creation. When you are sensitive to your own emotions – when you are clear – the inspiration of the universe will begin to flow and you will literally feel something beginning to awaken you from the inside. When I began to write down my vision all those years ago – the vision which was so influential in giving birth to Identity Network – as simple as it might sound, it just felt good. It feels good to daydream and to imagine future possibilities. Although, at the time, I had never had a single book published and had absolutely no connections to the publishing world, it felt good to dream. As I saw myself, within my mind's eye, writing and being published and coaching clients and ministering to audiences around the world, the feeling of inspiration was so strong. My friend, the feeling of inspiration you feel when beginning to think of the vision for your future is confirmation proof-positive that the future is within your reach. The feeling of the inspiration is, in some way, confirmation of the inner work of creation already beginning to swirl within you. So, before we delve into the deeper mechanics of writing down the vision for your life and making it plain, again I ask, what truly inspires you? What feelings would you like more of in your daily life? It's important to come to grips with the feeling now, because, if not, all of the material items in the world will mean very little to you. I work with clients day in and day out in my coaching sessions who used vision boards to attract into their lives great riches, properties across the globe, entire fleets of imported cars, and more love and romance than they even thought possible; however, many of them are still left feeling empty and void and without contentment. Why? Quite simply, because they never took the time to get in touch with the deeper emotions associated with the inner vision. For them, the extent of the vision was the material possessions themselves. Now, they have a series of bad relationships and some are even on the verge of bankruptcy already, simply because they never truly took the time to master their feelings. You see, when you begin to implement a vision board into your life to aid in visualization and manifestation, causing you to harness the power of the Law of Creation within your life, the universe will absolutely, one-hundred percent bring into your life all the material wealth you could possibly imagine. I'm certain of it. I see it happening daily. However, if you aren't prepared emotionally to handle the future you're building, then all the wealth in the world will never truly satisfy because you've begun your building project upon a foundation of sand. The scriptures are filled with principles and techniques which aid in building the future life. "Therefore, whosoever heareth these sayings of mine, and doeth them, I will liken him unto a wise man, which built his house upon a rock: And the rain descended, and the flood came, and the winds blew, and beat upon that house; and it fell not: for it was founded upon a rock. And everyone that heareth these sayings of mine, and doeth them not, shall be likened unto a foolish man, which built his house upon the sand: And the rain descended, and the floods came, and the winds blew, and beat upon that house; and it fell: and great was the fall of it." (Matthew 7:24-27) Without understanding the truest and most genuine intent of the heart, one will never fully be able to recognize the foundation which lies beneath the building. I want to lovingly encourage you to begin to see behind your vision, into the deepest thoughts and into the deepest and truest intention. The scriptures are replete with talk of intention and feeling. Since the true Kingdom of God which Jesus taught is, in fact, an *inner* Kingdom, it only stands to reason that in order to have a proper working knowledge of the Kingdom of God within, one must begin to do the work of uncovering their emotions prior to building their life. The writer of the Book of Hebrews says it in this way: "For the word of God is quick, and powerful, and sharper than any two-edged sword, piercing even to the dividing of soul and spirit, and of the joints and marrow, and is a discerner of the thoughts and intents of the heart." (Hebrews 4:12) My friend, this is why the prophetic voice is so vitally important within our daily lives. It's for this reason that we must learn to develop a great and lasting sensitivity to the inner voice of the Spirit within, rather than relying entirely upon our mind, will, and emotions, which can be so temporal and fleeting and so very often subject to change without notice. Before ever even choosing to put your pen to paper to construct a vision board, understand the life you wish to create by learning to recognize the feelings you are wanting more of. I assure you, when we place our minds and thoughts and the vision we set before our eyes into alignment, not only will we have whatever we desire, we will have it very quickly. Before we begin to discuss the mechanics of how a vision board works, I want you to be prepared to build. As I've said so very often, in my teachings and writings, thoughts really do become things. There is no question of this, as it's a scientific fact of physics. The true question is, "Will my life feel good when I create it?" Today, I want to encourage you to begin to dig a little deeper –

into the reality of the inner Kingdom of Heaven already within you, to begin to get in touch with the life you truly desire. The life of your dreams is already there, existing within your mind's eye. There's a reason you desire the things you desire. I want you to learn to recognize those reasons – those feelings and emotions – in order to become a more conscientious, careful creator and in order to master your own creative power within. I promise you, when you begin to put into practice the art of looking behind your vision and seeing into the intentions behind them, not only will you begin to manifest you dreams much more quickly when utilizing a vision board but you will, in turn, manifest with greater

ease.

THE CHANGING SCENERY

ᏣᎪᏋᎧ

"Behold I do a new thing," means to visualize or see something new God has in store for you that you have never seen before. – Jeremy Lopez

Vision is the substance of creation. Vision leads us. It sets before us a clear image of the road ahead and gives to us a blueprint of life, while, at the same time, reminding us of the creative power we possess to attain our desire. Vision reminds us that we are co-creators with God – that you and I have been entrusted with all the power of the Creator, in order to establish our decrees and our own desire within the earth realm. It would be impossible to speak of the importance of utilizing a prophetic vision board in order to create without taking a moment to recognize the role that vision truly plays within our lives. Suffice it to say, we are visual beings, and vision goes far beyond natural sight. Even the blind possess the Divine ability to imagine and to dream and to cast vision for their lives. Why? Because vision is a very powerful force of the Holy Spirit, not relegated simply to the natural eye. Vision is triggered within the soul – intrinsically interwoven into the deepest recesses of the mind, the will, and the emotion. In the King James Version of the Holy Bible, the word "vision" is used a total of seventy-nine times. The word "visions" is included a total of twenty-four times. There are seventy-three verses which include the word "vision." Perhaps one of the most haunting uses of the term within the Holy Bible is found within the

Book of Proverbs. "Where there is no vision, the people perish." (Proverbs 29:18) I can remember so often hearing this particular passage of scripture being expounded upon by the great theological minds and hearing it used to paint such a dark and dire picture for humanity. However, prophetically speaking, I choose, rather, to see it as an invitation to a brighter future. The word "perish," used within the context, is the Hebrew term "abad," meaning to become lost or broken or disconnected or separated. The original Hebrew term is used, quite literally, to denote the process of a journey toward a particular destination – toward an expected ending. As you can see, religion has capitalized on the word "perish" for centuries to cause fear and dread, when the literal meaning has always been a reminder for all to stay the course and to maintain their sense of direction. If we were to think of the life of our dreams as a destination, of sorts – a destination we are wishing to reach – the term "vision" begins to take on an entirely new and different meaning, does it not? We so often think of vision in such a mystical and ethereal way, often within the context of "dreams and visions." Although there is a very real component of the supernatural in regards to talk of vision, a vision, itself, is actually quite a very practical thing. It is an image – a picture –

either within the mind or within the earth. Actually, in truth, a vision is for, both, the earth realm and the spiritual realm, as you will soon see. A vision board, or dream board, is a tool to aid in the miracle of manifestation, and it's a tool that works one-hundred percent of the time. Prophetically speaking, the vision board is a means by which the internal vision – the vision within the mind's eye – is brought forth into the three-dimensional plane of the earth realm, causing "spirit to become flesh," in a sense. I've always loved the passage of scripture which details the healing of the blind mind. As a student of the deeper, hidden mysteries contained with the scriptures, I learned early on that in, both, the old and new testaments, there is much symbolism and typology. The detailing of the miracle by which Jesus healed the blind man shows the seeker that vision is not limited to merely natural sight. It further confirms to us that vision is more far-reaching than anything we can see with our natural eyes. However, interestingly enough, it also reveals to us that natural eyesight – what we place before our eyes on a daily basis – is vitally, vitally important. The tale of the miracle is depicted in the Gospel of Mark. "And he cometh to Bethsaida; and they bring a blind man unto him, and besought him to touch him. And he took the blind man by the hand, and led him out of the town; and when he had spit on his eyes, and put his hands upon him, he asked him if he saw ought. And he looked up and said. I see men as trees walking. After that he put his hands again upon his eyes, and made him look up: and he was restored, and saw every man clearly." (Mark 8:22-25) This passage of scripture, perhaps more than any other throughout the entirety of the gospels gives us, the readers, a depiction of the importance of vision – both the inner vision and the outer vision. From Genesis to Revelation, the scriptures contained within the Holy Bible are replete with passages which show us in great detail that when the Holy Spirit establishes an order or decree within the natural world – the world of flesh – there is an action which takes place within the spiritual world as well. In fact, even in the teaching behind "The Lord's prayer," the end result is for the will of God to be done on earth as it is in Heaven – showing us that there is a direct correlation between the will of God upon the earth and the will of God within the spiritual realm. However, in the passage detailing the healing of the blind man, we see something much, much differently. We see the principle reversed, in some way. Rather than seeing a command or decree immediately brought forth into the earth, we see, instead, a gradual process of manifestation – a gradual process of the inner vision becoming the outer vision. The passage also reminds us of the vast importance of sight and vision, as it relates to the process of manifestation and attraction. In the passage in the Gospel of Mark, we see the very detailed and precise mechanics of a literal creative miracle of manifestation. We are reminded that an inner vision – what we see within – must be brought forth into the literal, three-dimensional world of flesh and, secondarily, we are shown that it is the will of God for the vision to be clear – naturally and spiritually speaking. Jesus could have simply walked away when the man had received only a partial healing and said, "Well, at least it's better than it was." However,

Jesus was not content to leave the man behind with blurred vision. Instead, he prayed again until the man's sight was one-hundred percent completely restored. Not only is vision important, my friend, but *clear* vision is important. In fact, clear vision is vital to the process of manifestation. How very often have we attempted to create a life of fulfillment, only to fail because the vision we possessed for our lives hasn't been entirely clear? My friend, I say with all love and grace that one of the reasons you have yet to create a life you truly desire, which feels good for you, is because you've been creating with a blurry vision. You've been creating with a vision that hasn't yet been brought fully into focus. So, instead of making your decrees and commands to the universe from the realm of "I know," you've, instead been creating from the realm of "I think," and very little is happening. In other words, you've been content to settle for a blurry vision without complete focus! A young man once came to me and asked why his vision board wasn't working. I had explained to him in great detail how to create the vision board and exactly what to write down, based entirely upon what he had expressed was his truest and deepest desire. When he returned without any manifestation, the problem was immediately obvious to me. He hadn't been entirely truthful with himself about what he had been wanting. I immediately asked, "Are you sure these desires are what you truly want?" He replied, "I think so." And therein is the problem. You see, it's not good enough for you to have a vision for your future. You must have a *clear* vision for your future. Move from the realm of "I think" into the realm of "I know." Before we step into the Kingdom mechanics behind the actual creation of a vision board, I want to ask you, my friend, can you see your future clearly? I mean, truly? When you see the home and the car and the new relationships you want to attract into your life, what does it look like? Is it blurry? If so, you will never attract it into your life as quickly as you'd like to. I want to save you time and effort by teaching you this principle regarding vision which I learned early on in my years of study within the prophetic movement. "If you can see it, you can surely have it!" The issue, though, is that you have to be able to see it clearly. Bring your vision into focus, internally, first, and when you construct your vision board, the board will be the first tangible and literal physical illustration within the physical world of your desires coming toward you. Remember, a vision board is a tool which aids in manifestation, but the manifestation of your vision can only occur when your internal vision is clear and focused. I'll share much more about this soon; however, for now, suffice it to say that you must recognize the importance of clarity before ever even putting your pen to paper and long before ever even pasting photos of your dream home to a board. The vision must begin within, and it must be so real to you, even right now, that you will lose all doubt that your dreams can become a reality. Scripture speaks of bright futures – hope and an optimistic end. "For I *know* the thoughts I think toward you, saith the LORD, thoughts of peace, and not of evil, to give you an expected end." (Jeremiah 29:11) The Kingdom and all that it contains was established by a Creator with harnessed, focused intent. He *knew* what He wanted the end result to be, long before he ever created. In fact, as scriptures make plain, all things were created for His own good pleasure. Today, it's time to begin to see yourself as the creator of your own life and your own dreams. As I discussed in great detail within my book, *The Universe Is At Your Command*, the Kingdom is simply awaiting the decrees and commands of individuals in order to place those desires and dreams into motion around them. What happens for the most part, however, is that the universe is rarely ever given a clear blueprint, because most individuals aren't fully aware of what they truly desire. So, rather than decreeing to the universe the commands and desires of their hearts, they simply sit idly by waiting for God to do something. They, instead, pray prayers that lack heart and passion. They, instead, say, "Maybe it'll happen one day." My friend, when will you stop playing religious guessing games with your life? Religion has unfortunately convinced the whole of humanity that God is always attempting to play a game of hide-and-seek with individuals – sometimes we'll find fulfillment and sometimes we won't. Sometimes God will answer our prayers and sometimes He won't. What a sadistic view of the universe and of God. The literal power of creation's call is at your disposal at all times, and the catalyst of creation is your very own vision for your life. Viewing vision as an important aspect of a journey and as an integral part of a process of building, we can now safely say that the only thing keeping us from our truest and most contended lives is actually our own selves. When you begin to gather your materials for your vision board, have a clear vision already in place. Don't proceed until your blurry vision has been replaced with a clear vision – a crystal clear mental image within your mind's eye. Remember, this inner vision will serve as the basis we will soon be sending into the universe as we construct your vision board, together. Everything that you place upon your board will serve as the outward representation for your own, inner vision and your own, inner desire. Begin to see the vision clearly now, before ever gathering your supplies. My friend, let us put to death, once and for all, the blasphemous, religious notion that you and I must settle for lives with a blurry vision. Let's lay aside the weight of guilt and uncertainty which keeps us confined to the lives of mediocrity which the world around us has settled for. Imagine what must have gone through the mind of the blind man as Jesus passed by that day. For a moment, I want you to envision what that must have been like – what it must have felt like. With just one touch, the blindness began to leave and sight began to come. Out of nothingness – pitch black – came a little light and a few blurry images – men looking like trees. Having lived with blindness for so very long, I'm sure that even in that moment, even the little improvement must have seemed like quite a miracle. In all honesty, he must have been overjoyed to even have been given blurry vision. I mean even that was far better than total blindness. However, the miracle didn't end there. Jesus prayed again. Then came more light and even more clarity. The blindness totally left. He could see clearly. My friend, concerning the vision for your life, clarity matters. It is vital. As you begin to gather your materials for your vision board, recognize, first, that the vision needs to be clear in order to quickly and effortless manifest the desires of your heart into the natural, three-dimensional world around you. In order for spirit to become flesh, there must be illumination. The light must come. Could you imagine contractors and construction workers attempting to build with a blueprint that they were unable to see? So much would be left to chance. So much would be left to mere guess work. Well, in case you haven't realized it yet, the universe simply does not work that way. Above all, the Spirit does not work that way. Furthermore, vision does not work that way. Whenever the light shines in darkness –

whenever clarity comes to blurriness – miracles happen, and the entire universe will begin to move and to bend around you in order to accommodate your demands and decrees. Let's get started, shall we?

WRITE IT DOWN

෴

"To write your desire down on paper means that your heart must allow it to be known to the seen realm." – Jeremy Lopez

When the vision is known, the magic of creation begins to happen. Both, within the unseen realm and the seen realm – within the world of the Spirit and within the world of flesh and bone – the entire universe begins to bend and mold to conform to your decrees and desires. Once the vision is made known, all of creation begins to adjust itself to meet your demands. This is the most pure and simple explanation of The Law of Creation. As a powerful, thinking spirit who possesses all the power of the Godhead, you are daily placed into moments in which your desires and deepest thoughts are constantly being enacted around you. The problem, however, has always been that, for the most part, you've simply been unaware of your own creative power. Now that you've awakened, though, and now that you have the full knowledge of who you were before time even began – now that you understand your desires and your inner dreams – it's time to begin the process of creating the vision board. Gather your supplies. Vision boards can take on a variety of different sizes, shapes, and colors. In fact, no two vision boards should ever be alike, because your vision board should always be unique to you and to your own dreams. I've seen vision boards made upon poster boards, drawn upon construction paper, and even written down in prayer journals and scratched messily onto pieces of notebook paper. When I first began to realize the importance and necessity of writing down my visions and dreams, all those years ago, I honestly had no idea just how intricate and how detailed and how complex vision boards can become. Although I now have different boards of all shapes and sizes now hanging upon the walls of my office, for me, it didn't begin this way. In the very beginning, I simply wrote the vision down. A vision board is a reminder to you and to the Holy Spirit of your desires and dreams. Let's make it personal though. Your vision board is your daily reminder to yourself and to the Kingdom of your own desires and dreams. Your vision board is your decree to God. As I write these words, I have a dear friend whose younger sister, for years, has been interested in pursuing a career in modeling. My friend once said to me, "For as long as I can remember, that's all she's ever talked about." He explained to me how for years, she had spent so much money attending classes and pursuing auditions, only to never be given even a callback. "She started to feel hopeless," he said. "But then, she took control and everything changed within a matter of weeks." He explained to me that when she began to incorporate a vision board into her daily meditations, within weeks agencies began contacting her – agencies that she had never even reached out to! She was offered a modeling contract within a matter of days! When she began to mix the power of visualization with her dreams and desires, everything changed. One of the most important things to keep in mind when creating your vision board is that your vision board is just that – it's yours. These are your dreams you're writing down. These are your desires. The feeling and the images and the decrees and words used must all be completely unique to you, if your vision board is ever going to work the way you want it to. You can't expect to copy someone else's vision board and expect your dreams to come to pass. Why? Because your life was never meant to be lived to manifest the dreams and desires of other people. Your life should be lived to manifest your own dreams and desires. Desire is unique and vision is unique, so your vision board must also be uniquely your own. All too often, I see individuals, though very sincere with their intention, attempting to copy the designs of other vision boards. My friend, don't do it! Resist the urge and the temptation. Sure, it's alright to incorporate some of the certain design elements into your own creation – certain sizes and colors and fonts – however, your vision board should be designed in a way that reflects your very own personality. After all, your personality is a reflection of your very own soul, and it's the soul, itself, which plays a very vital role within the mystical and heavenly process of creation. Over time your vision boards will naturally begin to evolve and change and grow – as your vision begins to grow and take shape – but the process begins with one simple step: Write it down! My friend, as simple and as elementary as this step might seem, rest assured this step begins to unlock the supernatural power of creation in ways we can hardly even fathom. As I often share with my clients, "To write your desire down on paper means that your heart must allow it to be known to the seen realm." You might be thinking, "Jeremy, what does that mean?" Well, allow me to explain it this way. The moment you write down your vision upon paper, that's the very first moment it begins to be brought into the natural, three-dimensional world of flesh and bone. Up until the moment the pen is placed onto paper, the vision, though real, exists only within your mind's eye. Writing it down is the first step in actually bringing it into the earth realm. The moment you write the vision down, the vision is no longer confined to the inner recesses of the mind and the heart; it now exists upon paper in the natural world. It's concrete. The vision board can be seen with the natural eye, rather than the spiritual eye. It can be touched. I'm so often asked when the process of creation actually begins, and I often like to explain it in this way: "Creation begins the moment we have the first thought and desire, but the vision begins to become a reality the moment we write it down." When the pen is placed to paper, something quite extraordinary and supernatural – something metaphysical – begins to happen. The inner vision is brought into the natural world for the very first time in a very tangible and very real way. Over the past three decades of my work within the prophetic movement, I've witnessed, firsthand, the power of journaling. When someone is prophetically given a promise from the Holy Spirit, so often they feel compelled to write the promise down. This is, in truth, a form of a vision board. Even journaling can be used as the beginning stage of creating a vision board. So often, for those who do journal or keep a diary of their visions and dreams and spiritual inspirations, it's much easier to create a vision board because they're able to simply organize their journal entries onto the board in a more visual way. I know a man whose vision boards first began years ago in the form of what he, at the time, called "dream journals." Each night, at the end of the day, he would write down his feeling and hopes and dreams as a way to remind himself of the promises the Spirit had made to him. However, as he recounts, it wasn't until he began to change the wording within the diary that literally everything began to take shape. For years he had journaled in the form of prayers: "I want this to manifest." However, the moment he began to journal his entries as statements of facts – literal decrees and definitive mantras – everything began to evolve and finally take shape. Rather than writing "I want this," he began to take ownership of his dreams and declare, "I have this." Once the change was made from what he called "prayer" tense to "creation" tense, the entire world around him began to be uncovered in a new and refreshing way. Literally every prayer that he wrote in the form of a present truth came to pass within a matter of weeks! It was bizarre, really. I've found the same principle at work in my life though, and know, firsthand, why this happens. Though prayer is a very beautiful thing and I would never in any way attempt to discredit the power of prayer, we must remember that prayer, by definition, is simply communion with the Holy Spirit. So often, prayer is used as just another excuse for "wishful thinking," unfortunately. But when the tense and the tone are changed and declared from a position of already having, the universe recognizes it. So, instead of writing, "I want a new house," begin to write from a place of creation. Instead, make your decrees clear. "I have this new home." Remember, my friend, the universe in no way recognizes the feeling of lack or the feeling of going without. As I shared at great length in my book, *The Universe Is At Your Command*, the universe is one of abundance, not one of lack. The universe will always respond to the intention you set and to the demand you make within your own thoughts and intention. A vision board is essential because it helps to shift us from a place of wanting toward a place of already having. Let's take a moment to look at vision boards in a much more practical way, though. A vision board aids in the organization of our thought forms by providing us with a very detailed image to see and to recognize. In his book, *Images of Organization,* renowned sociologist and behaviorist Gareth Morgan says,

"An appreciation of the close relationship between thoughts and actions can help to create new ways of organizing." Would like to truly bring a sense of order and balance into your life? Would you like to, for perhaps the first time ever, abandon the constant feeling of being tossed about by all of your various dreams and desires? Well, the use of a vision board is paramount to this clarity. Write the visions down. By taking time to write down our visions, we are not only bringing our dream into the physical, natural world, but we are also bringing a newfound sense of organizational structure to our vision by finally giving it certain parameters and a concrete structure. No longer is the dream and vision a vague and innocuous idea, but rather it becomes a very tangible and definable image. It becomes organized – not merely some thought or desire floating about in the ether but, rather, a solid and tangible image to behold and to see and to touch. For me, my vision boards have always represented clarity and a sense of accomplishment. There are many who may view vision boards as nothing more than just images of wishful thinking; however, this is simply not the case. The vision board, because of the harnessed will behind it and the focused intention placed into it, is just as much of an accomplishment as anything else. In fact, in truth, the process of writing down the vision is actually a very big step, in itself, within the process of creation because just the act of writing down vision signals to the universe that we're serious about our own dreams. I often think of the process of writing down my visions in this way: "When I write down my vision and my desire, I'm saying to the universe, 'I'm ready.'" By even taking the beginning step to write down your vision and your dream onto a vision board, you are taking a very small step of faith and creating a very real, very tangible point of contact by which the energies of the Spirit are harnessed and brought forth into the three-dimensional plane of existence. Let me say it another way. By taking time to write down the vision, you are showing the universe that you have come into alignment with your desire and the moment you place pen to paper you are taking a leap of faith that demonstrates to the universe your active involvement. A vision board is your contract of creation with God. Imagine it as being your very own unique signature on the contract of your creation. When two parties enter into an agreement, in any capacity, in order to make the contract binding, there is paperwork and an exchange of signatures involved. The creation of a vision board – the writing down of your dreams – is your signature on a very real, spiritual contract between your very own soul and the powerful forces of creation in operation within the universe. When you create a vision board and write down your vision, you are quite literally saying to the universe, "I accept this agreement." Your vision board is your very own official seal upon the contract, in a sense. Within the Book of Habakkuk, as the prophet is given specific instruction to write down his vision and to make it plain for all to see, we see that he is also given, along with the instruction, a very real and otherworldly promise. The prophet Habakkuk is assured without question that the vision will come to pass, without delay. If one looks more deeply into the text contained within the scripture, one would find that the promise of fulfillment seems to be tied directly to the process of writing down the vision and making it plain for all to see. For a moment, I'd like to examine this passage of scripture more deeply, because I believe it details perfectly the spiritual and metaphysical behind-the-scenes mechanics of a vision board being put into practice. "And the LORD answered me, and said, Write the vision, and make it plain upon tables, that he may run that readeth it. For the vision is yet for an appointed time, but at the end it shall speak, and not lie: though it tarry, wait for it, because it will surely come, it will not tarry." (Habakkuk 2:2-3) In this particular passage, perhaps more so than in any other passage throughout the entirety of the scriptures, we see the metaphysical and transcendent power which is enacted the moment we write down our visions and dreams. The vision begins to speak for us. A vision written down quite literally calls out to the universe on our behalf. A written vision serves as a testament to our truest and deepest desire. A written vision will always come to pass. According to the words of the prophet of old, the vision will not lie. Whatever your vision is, the first and most vital element required to bring it into the physical world is to write it down. Would you believe it if I told you that even now, after having been tremendously blessed in my life and in my work all these years, even after having published successful books and garnered clients from across the globe, I still incorporate a vision board into my prayer and meditation daily? It's true. As long as the Divine breath – the *ruach* – is still within your physical body, you will continue to desire and to want. You will continue to still cast vision over your life and to dream. The wanting never ends, really. It never ceases. When dreams begin to manifest and come to pass, we begin to, then, dream other dreams, not only for our own lives but also for our families and friends and for those dearest to us. I want to encourage you today, my friend, take the first step into bringing forth your vision into the natural, physical world of flesh and bone – into the world where it can be experienced in the natural world – and write it down. When we make a contract with the universe, the entire world of the Spirit – the energies of the universe – begin to move around us to bring to pass our deepest desire. If you find yourself asking if this truly works, the answer is that you have no idea. Not only do I enjoy each day a life that I've attracted into for myself with the use of a vision board, but I see the power behind the vision board being used by my closest friends and even members of my very own staff. I don't believe it works; I know it works, from experience. Never were you ever meant to be the victim of the universe – merely some byproduct of universal cause and effect. No. Instead, you were always destined to recognize the truth of your own, creative power – the power of the Godhead – and harness it in order to create your own life. I know that for years, many of us – myself included – believed that life is merely a roll of the dice and that blessings come if we simply sit by and wait on God. Religion has done such a great disservice to humanity, I admit. Thankfully, though, when the awakening of the Spirit comes to us and when we are illuminated within, we begin to recognize who we truly are. We begin to take personal responsibility for our lives. We begin to recognize our own selves as the creators of our life experiences. My friend, today, is the day that you can take your dreams and begin to move them from the place within your heart and mind into the natural, three-dimensional world. Aren't you ready to begin to finally enjoy the car, or the boat, or the home, or the relationship you've been dreaming of? As good as it feels to dream, dreams can't be touched or experienced until they're drawn from the dream realm into the natural realm. This process always begins with a very simple step: Write it down.

MAKE IT PLAIN

ᚼ

"Write the vision, and make it plain upon tables, that he may run that readeth it." (Habakkuk 2:2)

When a vision comes, something begins to happen deep, deep within the recesses of the mind and heart. When a vision comes, so, too, does inspiration and hope. Hope truly does play such an important role within our daily lives that we so often fail to even recognize the important significance of this Divine aspiration. Hope is the calling card of the Holy Spirit. It is the reminder that there is more to come, although the feeling might seem quite contradictory to the present surroundings. In fact, if we were to be honest, hope is the reminder to us that our present circumstances are not our final resting place and that there is so much more to be enjoyed, experienced, and lived within. Hope keeps us moving onward into greater glories – both here and in the hereafter. Hope is never wasted. According to Romans 5:5, "Hope maketh not ashamed." In other words, it's hope that serves as the inner drive to move forward, to an expected, intended result – toward an exact target. However, there must be a target in mind. Hope, itself, is so much more than just wishful or positive thinking. I often like to think of hope as the driving force behind the desire we have which leads to creation. Think of it in this way, for a moment. Whenever you and I envision a different or better life for ourselves, we are, in essence, feeling an inner sense of hope, are we not? When you envision the new relationship that you've believed for or are praying for, is there not a sense of hope behind the desire? In fact, is hope not the basis of all prayer? "Now faith is the substance of things *hoped* for, the evidence of things not seen." (Hebrews 11:1) Hope is, in itself, evidence that a brighter future is awaiting us. In other words, the very fact that you and I can feel a sense of hope is proof-positive that a new creation is being enacted around us. But there must be a literal target in mind, as we begin the process of creation. We've seen how important the process of writing down the vision is when discussing the power of manifestation and how incorporating a vision board is the first step in bringing forth the inner vision into the natural world. We've seen how important the blueprint is when we begin the process of constructing our new lives, and we've seen how the entire universe begins to bend and to mold to meet our demands the moment we write the vision down. However, when creating a vision board, it isn't enough to simply write the vision down. We must make it plain. We must make it detailed. When creating a vision board, always remember that details matter. It isn't enough to simply say that you want the new home or the new car or the new relationship. Lean to make your vision more specific to your true desire. Decree your commands boldly in the Kingdom. Although no two vision boards are ever truly alike, because vision is always unique to the individual, based upon the expression of the individual soul, there is a common thread running through all successful vision boards: They are very detailed. I have a client that I coach who heads a very large Fortune 500 Company in the heart of New York City. He'll be the first to admit that his vision for his business began with the use of a vision board. In fact, he's even written a few New York Times bestselling books of his own, detailing the power of positive thinking. When he started the company in the basement of a small house that he was renting, more than twenty years ago, the vision board which sparked the launch of his company was nothing more than a single piece of poster board with a few lines of text and a few images. Today, though, his vision boards are often so intricate and so detailed that they span the walls of entire conference rooms and often have many, many sections. It's necessary, though, if you think about it, because as his success has grown over the years, so has his vision. Now, he is responsible for many different departments and he oversees more than one-thousand employees, so, of course, his vision boards will need to be a little more expansive and far-reaching. Now, on his vision boards, he has various time tables and charts and graphs, detailing the success he'd like to manifest within the next six months, the next nine months, and within the next year – each section and each time table containing very specific details for each department. Now, I'm in no way suggesting that your vision board needs to fill your entire home, and I'm not even attempting to suggest that the larger your vision board is the more quickly you will manifest your desires and your dreams into the physical world. What I am saying, though, is that details matter. The more specific your vision board is to your truest desire, the more quickly you will manifest the dream. When creating your vision board, think of what details are specific to you. If you'd like a new home and are creating it within your life, rather than just writing down that you'd like a new home, take time to make the vision more specifically detailed. Where would you like the home to be? Is there a certain neighborhood or city in which you'd love to find yourself living? What about the wall colors? What about the flooring? I mean, sure, you could always paint the walls and replace the flooring, but why not just be specific in your commands to the universe to begin with and save yourself the time and trouble? I was speaking with a young woman once who had learned to incorporate the vision board into her process of visualization and she reported to me that the moment God provided her with the home of her dreams, it was the exact home she had written down on her vision board, down to the exact color paint and the exact type of flooring. She said that the sellers, before placing their home upon the market, had even planted a beautiful flower garden filled with her tulips – her favorite type of flower. Even the tulips were yellow – her favorite color. I laughed that the universe had wanted to present her with a housewarming gift. You see, details matter greatly. When thinking ahead about the relationship you'd like to attract into your life, be very specific. What would you like for him to do for his career? Would you like for her to want children? Whether you've taken the time to realize it yet or not, these things matter. They're important. Far too often, marriage relationships end because of seemingly small, seemingly insignificant minor details. "He was always working, and it made me feel like he was choosing his career over the family." "I wanted children, and she didn't." Believe me when I say, I've heard it and seen it all before. Trust me, it's best to make the vision board plain now – make it detailed now – and save you the heartache and trouble. Get very specific. Get very detailed. Make it plain to begin with and leave no wiggle room for doubt. Remember, my friend, your vision board is your contract with the universe. It's your way of listing your decrees and commands. Sure, you could always recreate, but why would you want to? Why not be as specific as possible now, paying attention to every little detail? The Word of the Lord, spoken through the prophet Jeremiah, declares, "For I know the thoughts that I think toward you, saith the LORD, thoughts of peace and not of evil, to give you an *expected* end." (Jeremiah 29:11) This passage of scripture, perhaps more than any other throughout the entirety of the ancient scriptures details the importance of having a target – an expected end result – in mind when planning ahead. Today, I ask you, what are your expectations concerning your vision? What are you expecting, where your vision is concerned? Once you begin to write down your vision and make it plain, I want to lovingly encourage you to begin to set your heart like flint toward the expected outcome. As you begin to feel an inner hope rising up within you, recognize that this inner hope is, itself, proof of the creative power already working for you. I often tell my clients in life coaching sessions, particularly when discussing the vision board, "When you feel yourself beginning to lose hope, just go back and add more details." As simple and as elementary as this principle might sound, I promise you, I've found that nothing inspires hope for the future quite like pondering the many intricate details of the life awaiting you. There was once a young man who had for months been wrestling with a call into full time ministry. Being passionate for the things of the Spirit from an early age, he recognized early in life that he would never truly find satisfaction until he surrendered to his calling. And so he did. To his surprise, speaking engagements began to pour in and he found himself booked months in advance at churches and venues throughout the southeast. Still, though, he felt that there was more just ahead. To him, it had begun to feel as though he had hit a plateau. It was at this point that he began to incorporate a vision board into his daily prayer and meditation. When it seemed as though very little was happening around him and when he felt himself beginning to feel hope seemingly beginning to dwindle and the vision for more opportunity seeming far off, each night he made it a practice to begin adding more detail to his vision board. His dream was to launch out into television and radio ministry in order to reach a larger audience with his message, and as he began to add more detail to the vision board, he found himself surprising even himself. He added very specific dates as mile markers, decreeing to the Kingdom and to the Holy Spirit that within a very specific time table he was expecting to reach his target. Would you believe that within a period of time, less than forty-eight hours away from his target date, he received an unexpected call from a woman who had once attended one of his events and she offered him, down to the very cent, the amount of money he needed to launch his television ministry? I know this man well, and he, to this day, attributes the power of the miracle to the principle of being specific. In my own life, I've seen this time and time again, with my work in the prophetic. For decades, I've counseled and coached individuals, just like him, to become more specific with their visions and to begin taking control of their own dreams and desires. My friend, I know from decades of experience of my work within the prophetic movement that something powerful and miraculous begins to happen the moment we begin to get specific with our vision. Consider the details of your vision a way of taking ownership – taking stock – in your investment. Adding details – highly detailed specifics – is your way of saying to the Holy Spirit that you're taking ownership of your dreams and crafting them to make them uniquely your very own. Today, more than three decades after I created my first vision board and began to incorporate into my life the power of visualization, I continue to still see the miraculous power of creation beginning to be enacted the moment I begin to get very specific. These days, even my staff often marvels at just how quickly my dreams begin to become a reality the moment I begin to add detail to my vision boards. At first, they simply couldn't believe it; however, it's happened so frequently that now they just recognize it as a part of my daily life. My friend, you simply wouldn't believe it, even if I told you, the number of times, I've found myself desiring something – either for my own, personal life or for the outreach of Identity Network – and within hours of placing it upon the vision board, I will often receive a phone call from either a new client or from an investor or from a publisher, exclaiming that they were feeling "led" to reach out to me to make me an offer. As bizarre and as frightening as it might seem, I've learned to accept it as just part of the power of creation working within my life. You have that same creative power – the power of the Godhead which formed the worlds within the cosmos – and you have a responsibility to take ownership for your creation. Part of learning to take ownership means learning to become very specific about the target – the *expected* end – in sight. After I received my first publishing deal all those years ago and found myself literally catapulted onto the world's stage in ministry, I quickly realized that the same universal principles that had so radically changed and shifted my life were principles that needed to be shared with the world. You see, the life of your dreams is not merely a matter of being in Divine favor. Please understand me when I say that I absolutely believe in the power of the Divine favor of God; however, even more so, I believe in the power of taking control of my life and using the power God has given me to create the world I choose, though the Holy Spirit. As the scriptures reveal, literally all things were made by Him and for Him, for no other reason than for the purposes of His own good pleasure. In the very beginning, at Creation, God looked upon His matchless handiwork and exclaimed that it was "good." Can you, as the Creator of your very own life, having been given dominion in this earth realm, say the same about your own life and your own visions which have led you to where you now find yourself? Can you literally, honestly say, in truth, that your life feels good? Can you say that you literally take pleasure in your life? If not, well, then there's no time like the present moment – the NOW moment – to begin adding very specific details to the vision of your life. If you've followed my work for any amount of time, I'm sure you've probably heard me say, either in my writings or at my conferences, that the Lord will do nothing else. So often people hear me say this and they feel a sense of shock. "Jeremy, how could you say such a thing?" Well, allow me to explain. The Word of the Lord through the prophet Amos declares, "Surely the Lord GOD will do *nothing*, but he revealeth his secret unto his servants the prophets." (Amos 3:7) Yes, the Lord is active and yes the Lord is alive and well; however, hear me when I say that all power has been given unto us. The literal power of creation has been entrusted to us, and it is up to us to manifest the power of the Godhead – the creative power of the universe – in our own, daily lives and spheres of influence. My friend, this is what it means to establish the Kingdom in the earth realm. After all, was that not the heartfelt prayer of Jesus, himself as he taught his disciples to pray? That the Kingdom would come to earth, and be established here just as it is in Heaven? My friend, I learned years ago, through much trial and error and through my own year so experience and thankfully by my own spiritual awakening that if you're waiting for God to create for you a better life, you will die in your hopelessness. The scriptures are filled with passage after passage of deeper mysteries and patterns and universal principles detailing The Law of Attraction and The Law of Creation, reminding us all of the vast importance of personal responsibility. Whether you've followed my work and my ministry for years, since the beginning, or you've just seemingly stumbled upon my work for the very first time when researching the power of The Law of Attraction, my sincere and heartfelt prayer for you is this: That you would begin to take ownership of your vision. Begin to take stock in your own future, in your own life, and set your own targets to be achieved and attained. The vision board is vitally important in the process of creation and miraculous manifesting because it reminds us of an expected end in sight. The expected end is that of your very own choosing, so learn to get specific.

METAPHYSICS IN CREATION

ᘓᘏᘛ

In the beginning, there was the force of creation. This force existed in the form of a thought, and that thought form harnessed the inner vision of the Creator. When speaking of the immense power of creation being enacted the moment we place pen to paper and begin to write down the visions for our lives, upon a vision board, I would be remiss if I neglected to take you on a journey into the deeper recesses of the spiritual world of the inner Kingdom of God. It is, after all, the power of the Holy Spirit which is behind all that we can see or think or do. It is the power of the Holy Spirit – the great architect of all that is – which triggers us to begin to uncover the deepest and truest desires of our own souls. Since discussing at great length the powerful force of inspiration in my book *Creating With Your Thoughts*, I've literally found myself bombarded with correspondence asking if I would go even deeper into an explanation of the mechanics at play behind the process of visualization, as visualization relates to the thought forms which flood our minds, daily. In *Creating With Your Thoughts*, I discussed for the first time with my readers the transcendent universal principle of what is known scientifically as "The Observer Effect." As mystical as this concept might seem, at first thought, it is simply a scientific principle, constantly at work, at all times. In fact, the principle is so intrinsically interwoven into the fabric of creation that we often miss the deeper truth of the principle and rarely ever even take the time to recognize the true mechanics of what is truly taking place the moment we see something – be it in the natural world or in the realm of the Holy Spirit. The moment we see something – whether externally with our natural sight or internally within our own souls – a mechanism of creative force begins to become enacted instantaneously. As I've shared before, you and I are not our thought forms; we are the observer of our thought forms. In other words, you and I are not really what we think; we are the one watching – observing – what we think. The instant a thought passes into our minds, there is always, with each thought, the triggering of a certain visual image. As we are created to be visual beings, there is quite literally no escaping this scientific truth. If I were to describe to you, in great detail, a beautiful, lush field of flowers – flowers of all color – it would be impossible for you to not see that image within your mind's eye. In fact, the very moment you read the description of the field, your mind began to work to conjure the image internally for you to see within your mind. When the thought came and flashed onto the screen of your mind, did you all of the sudden become the field of flowers? No. Of course not. How absurd. You were merely looking on and observing it. The same is true of literally all thought and all visualization. You and I are the observers. In a very Divine way, you and I have been created to be visual beings. We enjoy sight and imagery. How very bland would the world be without color and the many different sights and scenes of life? As I've said before, even the blind man possessed an inner vision of the world, internally. Allow me to use a rather worldly example to further illustrate this point and this principle. Each year the pornographic industry amasses billions of dollars in revenue. With every purchase of a video and with each download, the desire to lust becomes even more overwhelming, further adding to the bottom dollar. Why? Because, instinctually, the human body is designed to in some way be drawn further toward what it sees visually. In a May 2014 article in Huffington Post, written by Elmwood D. Watson, the following statistics were given regarding pornography. At the time, it was estimated that annually the pornographic industry amasses more than 13 billion dollars and that the amount seemed to be consistently climbing. At the time, 50% of religious men and 20% of religious women claimed that they were literally addicted to pornography. 91% of people who identify themselves as religiously "fundamentalist" are 91% more likely to look at pornographic material. The article detailed the findings of a survey conducted by the Barna Group, which shared the following figures. 79% of men between the ages of 18 and 30 view pornography monthly. "Christian" men are watching pornography while at work at the same rate as the national average. 33% of those who view pornographic material either think that they have developed an addiction or are unsure if they have become addicted. I share these findings with you to simply say, quite emphatically, we are visual beings and our visualizations are more powerful than we can ever even fully describe. You see, something internally begins to happen the moment we see an image. There is, in a sense, a very real internal triggering of the questioning of desire. "Does this feel good or not?" If the answer to the question is "yes," then the brain begins to become molded and reshaped to create even more of a desire. Scientifically speaking, where cognitive function is concerned, the principle of "neural plasticity" shows us this even more. With each thought and with each desire – triggered by certain images – the brain is literally reshaped and becomes quite literally hardwired to want and to desire more of that which feels good. Addictions are formed because of this. Might I add, addictions can also be broken because of this with a simple shifting of the visual being looked upon. Once, years ago, I was traveling in Los Angeles for a book tour. I had just left LAX and was on the freeway when, just up ahead of me, there was a horrific accident, as a speeding car crossed the median and crashed into oncoming traffic. I watched in absolute horror and panic as the driver of the speeding car was ejected onto the freeway, only moments before both vehicles involved quickly burst into flames. There were no survivors. As horrifying as it was, I simply couldn't look away. It was almost as if, regardless of how violent the scene – knowing full well that death had occurred – I was unable to pull my eyes away from the carnage. I'm sure you've heard the expression, "It was like a train wreck; I couldn't look away?" Well, it was like that. There's a literal truth to that expression, whether we realize it or not. Partly because of the fact that we are designed to visualize and to see and, even more so, because traumatic events witnessed are quite literally hardwired into the human body physically. This is why PTSD can be experienced just as equally by those who witness a trauma as those who endure the trauma firsthand. "The Observer Effect" states, quite simply, that when we change the way in which we view, that which is being viewed will, in turn, begin to change forms. This metaphysical principle of change is paramount to the discussion of vision boards. You see, being hardwired to be visual beings, the moment we begin to make a practice of placing certain images before our eyes, we begin to, in turn, rewire the inner circuitry of our brains. My friend, this is a scientific fact. With each prolonged image, new neural pathways are created within the brain to further promote a kind of dependence upon the image. We desire it more. We feel we need it more. As a result, feelings and emotions change. Because of this change, the object itself begins to take on an entirely new and different, more significant meaning. As you can probably now begin to see, there's a very real reason why the Spirit inspired me to entitle this book about vision boards *Creating Your Soul Map*. By utilizing a vision board in your own process of creation you are, quite literally, mapping out your own future by placing before your very own eyes the images of your desire. Your vision board and the images and words upon it are an extension of your own energy. The triggering of the inner desire you feel when seeing the vision board further propels the feeling of desire, as new neural pathways are formed with each passing glance. Metaphysically speaking, each time you look upon your vision board, you are literally allowing the vision to become a tangible part of your everyday life. By observing the image, you are, in essence, bringing the image to life. Although we are not our thoughts and are, instead, the observer of our thoughts, the truth is that thought truly do become things, in that they become tangible expressions of our own, harnessed focused intent. This, my friend, is why meditation is so very important. I've always loved the way in which Jewish mystics describe the process of creation. According to teachers of Jewish mysticism, the moment something is spoken of or written about three times, that thing becomes part of the natural, physical world. Jewish teachers refer to this as *chazakah.* I've seen this principle at work, myself, over the years. I often am able to manifest my dreams and desires even more effortlessly and quickly when I write them down in sequences of threes. Once, just to put the principle to the test, I wrote down upon one of my vision board, "The publisher will contact me by noon on Friday. The publisher will contact me by noon on Friday. The publisher will contact me by noon on Friday." You're probably wondering, "Well, Jeremy, did it work." I received the call at 11:30am on Friday, so you be the judge. As miraculous and as metaphysical as the power of creation is within the life of an individual, the true power lies within the science behind "The Observer Effect." Because of the creative power constantly being enacted through our visualizations, you and I bring into the natural world of flesh and bone exactly what we continue to see. It's the power of the Kingdom at work. The word metaphysical is based in the root term "meta," meaning "beyond." When we are speaking of the metaphysical world, we are speaking of the world that it "beyond" the physical, natural world. When we begin to incorporate the vision board into our practice of visualization, we are making a decision to open the door to the world of the Spirit, and there is a very real and transcendent power that begins to take effect. I often think of the vision board as simply another "point of contact." In the charismatic and Pentecostal circles of Evangelical Christianity, there are often certain points of contact that are used as points of activation – from prayer cloths to prayer shawls to prayer journals and even, to some degree, the laying on of hands. These points of contact serve as points of activation through which creative power flows, based upon the expectation of the recipient and the intention behind the action. Remember the passage within the scriptures that depicts Jesus healing the woman who had suffered from the issue of blood? This passage is detailed within the 9th chapter of the Gospel according to Matthew. The woman had said to herself that if she could only press through the crowds to touch the hem of his garment, she would be healed. When the miracle happened, Jesus said to her that it was her own faith that had made her whole. Yet he felt the power leave him, as she touched the hem of his garment. This is an illustration of the spiritual world of the inner Kingdom of Heaven – the metaphysical world – at work in daily operation. The power which activates the world of the Holy Spirit is the power of intention. When creating the vision board as a point of contact in manifesting your dreams and desires, you are literally making a decision to place your intention into the desired outcome – the expected end result – and are preparing yourself to receive the manifestation. Again, this is far more than just a mere sense of wishful thinking. The activation of intention goes far, far beyond that. The activation of intention through the use of points of contact opens the door to the power of the Spirit by the utilization of expectation. The woman who had suffered from the issue of blood could have just as easily said to herself, "If I can just shake his hand and meet him, then I'll be healed." You see, the point of contact truly was insignificant. The point of contact was determined by her own expectation, based upon what she had said to herself – the commitment that she had, in her own mind, made to the universe around her. By creating a prophetic vision board, you are saying to yourself, "I have this now within my life and this will be my outcome," and – as a result, the power of the Spirit rises up to greet you in your

133

proclamation to ensure that your endeavor comes to pass just as you had intentioned. I discuss much more of the science behind this within my books *The Universe Is At Your Command* and *Creating With Your Thoughts*. Today, my friend, I want to encourage you to begin to see the world of the Spirit – the realm of the I AM – in a much more transcendent and larger way. The miraculous is always the result of a partnership between two words – the world of flesh and the world of the Kingdom. In order to begin to possess a proper understanding and working knowledge of life within the Holy Spirit, it is vital that you first recognize that you have a very real role to play within the creation process. You, as the creator of your life experiences, are setting the intention, the parameters, for the creative work. You are deciding the end result of your own decrees, and the Spirit, upon hearing your decrees and seeing your harnessed, focused intention, rises to meet you. When you learn to recognize that it is the intention behind the action which unleashed the power of creation, you will see physical healing, financial prosperity, and greater abundance. A vision board is a beginning step toward the discovery of the greater realms of the Holy Spirit operating around you at all times. The power does not reside in the board. The board is merely another point of contact. The power

resides within your own Self.

SPIRITUAL THERAPIES

ଓଞ୍ଚ

T oday, like never before, the world in which we live and experience life seems to be becoming more and more filled with stress and an overwhelming sense of hopelessness. I see it daily within my work and each day hear countless stories from beautiful souls expressing a desire to simply give up on their dreams and visions. As you well know, now, more than ever, it's so easy to give place to the inner feeling of hopelessness and despair. In fact, one needs to only turn into the nightly news to see what seems like a world in such disarray and chaos. I in no way seek to suggest that there aren't very real ills which exist in the natural world around us; however, I want to suggest to you, prophetically, that the outside world isn't getting worse, it's simply that the perspective of humanity is shifting away from the inner world of the Kingdom of Heaven. The truth of the matter is that, although, the feeling of hopelessness might seem to be becoming more apparent and more overwhelming, there's truly nothing new under the sun and it's still the same world it's always been. May I lovingly and respectfully encourage you to remember this, my friend? Why do I make mention of the outside world seemingly being in such disarray? Because it is paramount to the process of creation for you to understand the importance of personal responsibility – the importance of taking responsibility for your own life, in spite of the happenings of the world around you. It's so very easy to blame others. To say that it's because of "them" that life is the way it is. To some degree, that may be true. However, it is not for "them" to change your life. It is, rather up to you. In my coaching work these past three decades, I've seen, firsthand, the impact of a lack of responsibility. I've seen marriages end because of it. I've seen multi-billion dollar businesses crumble and declare bankruptcy because of it. I've seen millions of individuals settle fort the mundane and the mediocre status-quo because of it – refusing to better themselves. Furthermore, I've seen, time and time again, individuals, just like you, give up on their dreams and visions of a brighter life simply because they've stopped short of their own manifestation. As tempting as it might be, my friend, don't do it. Don't you dare do it. I say to you, prophetically, that if you stop short of your vision and if you look away – allowing your gaze to be shifted away from the internal vision to the outside chaos – you will die in mediocrity and you will accomplish nothing. You will stay exactly where you are. You will never begin the business. You will never buy the new home. You will never own the new car. You will never enjoy the new and loving relationship which will bring true satisfaction and contentment. Why? Because of the ills of the outside world? No. Because of your own neglect of your dreams. As a highly successful life coach and new thought leader with a worldwide clientele, I can assure you, my friend, the reason you are not living the life of your dreams is no one's fault but your very own. I say that with all love and all grace and all respect for your life experiences. The Republicans didn't do it. The Democrats didn't do it. Your ex didn't do it. The church down the road didn't do it. Your boss didn't do it. You did it. You are now in a state of being that you, yourself, have manifested. The most essential part of life coaching is the element of personal responsibility. In sessions, day in and day out, I prophetically encourage individuals, just like you, to become "un-stuck" in their thinking – encouraging them to shift from an old paradigm to a new way of life. This comes solely through personal responsibility. Do you truly want a better and more prosperous life? Then it's up to you to get it. No one else. I don't say that to be harsh or critical of your experiences. Were you dealt a few unfair breaks? Absolutely. Was the pain and heartbreak real? Absolutely. But it's a new day. Today is a new day, and this is a brand new moment. This is the NOW moment. Miraculous turnarounds always begin in the NOW. My friend, in case you have yet to realize it yet, the people that you've been waiting on for help, they're trying to better their own lives. Will you begin to do the same for your own soul? I remember speaking to a young woman once – a beautiful, single mother of two small girls. She felt completely hopeless and so alone in the world. After her husband of five years had decided to leave her and the children for another, even younger woman, she found herself asking, "What's the point?" The pain was real. The discouragement was real. The sense of hopelessness was real. For three years, she sat by the phone, hoping and praying that he'd call, admitting that he'd been wrong and that he still loved her more than anything. The truth of the matter, though, was that was never going to happen. While she was spending her days and nights waiting by the phone for him to admit the error of his ways, he was happily traveling the world with a younger woman, seemingly without a care in the world. In many ways, the death of her relationship had become the death of her. To her, it seemed that there was no more life left to enjoy. When she began to incorporate a vision board into her visualization and meditation practice, it would have been so, so very easy for her to have requested the reconciliation of her marriage – decreeing and demanding that the universe bring him back to her. I have no doubt that the universe would have obliged her command. However, when coaching her, the Spirit said to her, "When creating a future, never look back." Rather than creating a vision board based entirely upon old, past experiences of memories long-since gone, she crafted a vision board with her own, best interest at heart. Today, her life is completely different. Having worked in spirituality all these year, I prefer to take a spiritual approach. I honor the work of doctors within the medical profession, and, in truth, there is a place for the medical profession. However, in life coaching, it is the voice of the Holy Spirit that must always resonate. "What is the Spirit saying?" When implementing the vision board into your life, keep this question always at the center of your work. "What is my own soul saying to me?" I want to share with you six principles of therapy and self-care that I've found can be attained through the use of the vision board. When you begin to feel hopeless and without an inner drive or when you begin to look back, rather than forward, remember these six principles:

- A vision board helps us to follow through with our goals by allowing us to visually see our goals. You will attract what you see.

- A vision board will show you what can become reality. A vision board drives out the darkness and forces you to see "hope."

- A vision board encourages the dreamer within to emerge

- A vision board aids in organization. The vision board is your actual brain, in written form.

- A vision board will prophesy to you continuously of what will be and of what is to come.

- A vision board keeps the "I AM" nature of who you are in view, allowing you to see your true Self.

By utilizing the vision board, you are literally keeping the "I AM" of who you are in sight, rather than dwelling within the realm of "I WAS." One of the greatest tools for spiritual self-care that I have ever seen is the vision board. I say this because I've seen literal miraculous turnarounds within the lives of individuals, just like you, who at one time seemed to be so very stuck in old paradigms and patterns. I can't even begin to recount to you the number of times I've heard an individual say, "The vision board was like therapy for me." I hear it almost daily. In fact, I've heard it so often, I've sometimes wondered why this is the case. Then, through the Holy Spirit, I realized the answer: it encourages forward momentum. It reminds us to keep pressing onward into new and greater glories, rather than sitting idly by and hanging onto old memories of the past. My friend, your past experiences were very real and, yes, they served a purpose. However, the season has changed. With the season change must also come a paradigm shift within the mind, in order for you to begin to enjoy the NOW moment. A vision board aids in the process of forward momentum because it sets before our eyes the new and bright future ahead. It reminds of a place called "Hope." Spiritual self-care is vitally important within the life of an individual, regardless of his or her faith or creed or dogma, because it provides a constant sense of refreshing. Each day, as I rise to greet the new morning, I feel so overwhelmed with a new sense of inspiration. I now enjoy a life that I once only dreamed of. Now, the life that I once dreamed is now my current reality. The space that once, years ago, existed only in my mind's eye, is now a literal physical space that I enjoy each day in the natural world. So many people often ask, "Jeremy, do you ever have a bad day?" Well, of course, I'm only human, just like you. However, I've learned over the years that "good" and "bad" are both simply matters of perspective. Remove the word "bad" from your vocabulary if you're ever going to live a life of abundance and enjoy your own creative power. Sure, there are days when I feel stress and the feeling of being overwhelmed because of the demands of the day; however, whenever I begin to feel a sense of stress building within

151

me, I take a moment and remind myself, "This is the life I've chosen to create." In an instant, I immediately recognize how far I've come and the sense of stress is replaced with a sense of overwhelming gratitude and thankfulness to God and to the universe around me. My friend, there is absolutely nothing more exhilarating than awakening to a new day and learning to view it as an adventure. If you aren't enjoying the creation of your day, simply take a moment to recalibrate and recreate. Start fresh. When you are clear inspiration will flow, and when inspiration comes, so, too, does the power of God and effortless manifesting. It's important to always remain cognizant of the creative force within, even when seeing the images of a seemingly chaotic world externally around me. The Holy Spirit spoke to me years ago and reminded me that I'm simply to do my part. Nothing more and nothing less. All that the Spirit is asking is that you do your part and act responsibly with the creative power of the Law of Creation and The Law of Attraction entrusted you and that you have faith in God. The rest will always work itself out, I assure you. You see, by changing your creation of your own day, within your own life, first, you are, in turn, beginning to change the entire world. You and I are drops in the ocean, but are always at all times connected to the entirety of the ocean.

We are all connected. You've perhaps heard it said that if you truly want to change the world, start by changing yourself. Well, prophetically speaking, this is a true statement. Stand for justice and walk humbly in love and always give freely, but how very often have we deprived others of their own creation by attempting to "save the world?" I learned early on that success is unique to the individual and creation is a very personal thing. Again, I say, only you can truly change your life. When speaking to clients from throughout the world, I encourage them to use the vision board not only to create the lives of their dreams but, also, because by using the board, they are in turn learning to feel the flow of their own inner inspiration within their own lives. Never underestimate the power of responsibility. I can remember years ago, when I was first starting out in ministry, so very passionate and hungry to change the world. If you're familiar with the charismatic and Pentecostal background, I'm sure you're well aware of the mindset I'm referring to. Always fighting against devils. Always trying to change those who weren't like us. Always trying to convince someone that our ways were the right ways and that they were going to be damned if they didn't see it our way. Always believing that we were superior to others. It's such pride and such ego, really. Religion neglects grace.

In truth, religion is exhausting, isn't it? It's so draining. There's really no abundant life in religion, only the sense of constant struggle and an endless waiting game. It's like a game of roulette, if we were to be completely honest. It teaches that blessing and favor are reserved only for the select few and that God, in His omnipotence, is constantly looking on and being ever-selective in who to bless and who to curse. Then Jesus came. Thankfully. With his revelation of the inner Kingdom came also a new and illustrious paradigm of thought – that the glory which existed within the Godhead had been freely given to us. What a relief. Today, I choose to create effortlessly and without struggle, because I know, prophetically, that it is the Divine birthright of all humanity to possess the creative power of the Godhead. The Holy Spirit is always guiding and leading into truth. Now, I realize, I don't have to change the world; I only need to enjoy my own creation and when I do, others are seeing the glory of the Christ in me. If my teachings and principles help others, wonderful. I want to be a blessing. If they choose not to believe, then that isn't my responsibility. My friend, how often have we literally stressed ourselves out attempting to change others? By doing so, we are disconnecting ourselves from the limitless and abundant flow of creative force and we are dulling the sense of inspiration within us. I refuse to do it. Instead, I choose, simply, to be a conscientious creator of my own life. My sincere and heartfelt prayer for you is that you would begin to do the same. Begin making it a practice, daily, to take time to refresh and to spiritually self-care. The vision board helps in this, more than one might consciously realize. My friend, I literally could not imagine going through life without my vision boards. I simply couldn't do it. There's just something otherworldly and inspiring that takes place within me when I wake each day and look around my home and see the images of my dreams. Because I'm constantly setting the vision and the dream before my eyes each and every day, I'm constantly being encouraged to live from the realm of inspiration and from the realm of abundance. It's very difficult to be stressed and overwhelmed and anxious when before my eyes, constantly are the images of the dreams and visions for my future. I've arranged my home – my personal solace – in such a way that the visions for my future are always set before my eyes, regardless of where I turn. It's literally impossible for me to even walk through my home without seeing something that inspires me. I have it that way intentionally and by design, because I know, firsthand, that thoughts become things and that the image I set before me triggers the inner power of creation, as I call my dreams and visions into the natural world. Part of spiritual self-care is positioning the life around you in such a way that you feel a continuous flow of inspiration. People often find it humorous when I say to them that if they would spend as much time looking at their vision boards as they do the pile of bills on the table that they would begin to have more money to pay the bills. Though I say that laughingly, it's absolutely true and I mean it wholeheartedly. My friend, I've seen it happen too many times to doubt its truth. Are payments and bills part of natural life within the physical world? Of course. However, when we begin to incorporate a vision board into our lives we are stepping out into the world of the supernatural. Few things are more depressing than the feeling of lack and loss. Well, as we've discussed, our feelings and emotions matter because they serve as the fuel behind our creation process. Why have your home or your office organized and arranged in such a way that your bills are constantly in view on your kitchen table, when your kitchen table should be a place to enjoy peaceful meals? Yes it matters. What you are setting before your eyes is keeping you locked into the patter of debt because it's what you are continuing to create. Arrange your home in such a way that you are constantly feeling inspired. I'll share more about this later; however, please know that what you set before your eyes daily is having a tremendous impact upon what you are creating. Set the vision before you at all times. Arrange your vision boards and dream boards so that when you awaken to a new day, you're able to see your future life. Position your promises in such a way that all throughout the day you are constantly being bombarded with flashes of inspiration as you see the life of yours dreams. I was coaching a young man once who had found himself going daily to a job that he hated. "It feels like the life is bring drained out of me," he exclaimed. I instructed him to create a small, inconspicuous vision board that could be placed within a drawer of his desk in his office, so that randomly throughout the day, when he was in need of a feeling of inspiration he could look at it. After following my instructions, he reported back to me within six weeks with the following news: "Two weeks after I started using the vision board in my desk, my boss who had constantly been making my life miserable made the announcement that he would be resigning from the company. Two weeks later, I was offered a position in another company, doing what I love and making three times what I was making before." You can't tell me that it doesn't work. I've seen it firsthand and have heard far, far too many testimonies. If you now find yourself living a life that literally feels as if the life is being sucked from you by vampires, take time each day to self-care and learn to refresh yourself with thoughts of inspiration. This is more vital than perhaps any other universal principle. Your feelings matter greatly, as they are truly the gauge of your creation. Although we live within a world which seem to continue to stress the "necessary evil" of working jobs that we hate and living lives that aren't satisfying, why not begin to recognize, today, that you are worthy and deserving of the abundant life which Jesus spoke of? After all, are you not a child of the

Creator? Are you not living a life within the Kingdom, just as He promised? The very moment you can begin to see that you and you alone are responsible for the creation of your life, you will begin to develop a much more heightened sensitivity to the energies of creation within you. You will never again look to others to give you the sense of fulfillment that you, yourself, have been fully capable of creating, all along. It truly is a beautiful and remarkable adventure, this thing called "life," when you are able to see it as your very own miracle. You are both, the architect and the builder. I'm here to remind you that construction is underway. You simply need to recognize it.

THE MIND BODY

CONNECTION

ॐ

As we begin to delve even more deeply into the spiritual mechanics – the metaphysics – behind the vision board, it's important to remember that all creation is enacted from within. When Jesus spoke of the inner Kingdom of Heaven, he was speaking of a very present reality of constantly-flowing, ever-present creative power. He was speaking of a very present power and not some reality-existing far-off in the distance, awaiting a future time and being reserved only for the select few. Many people often feel a sense of shock when they learn that I have images of Gandhi upon my vision board in my home. Many exclaim, "Jeremy, that seems so very 'new age' and extreme." I love the work of Gandhi, not only because of the spirituality that he represented and the all-encompassing love that he promoted through his work but, also, because he is considered to be one of the greatest thought-leaders of all time. Many are surprised to know that Gandhi was actually a lover of Jesus. It was, in fact, Gandhi, who famously said, "I like your Christ, I do not like your Christians. Your Christians are so unlike your Christ." How true, unfortunately. Although my many critics would often argue otherwise, the truth of the Kingdom of Heaven which Jesus spoke of is actually much, much more miraculous than the religious orthodoxy of westernized Christianity would care to admit. So often I was told, when first stepping out into public ministry, "Jeremy, just preach Jesus." Well, the truth of the matter, my dear friend is that it is impossible to love Jesus without teaching what Jesus taught, and Jesus taught that the Kingdom of Heaven resides *within* and not in a church building somewhere or within a religious dogma. The moment Christianity can finally recognize Christ, everything will change, and the miraculous will continue to flow once more within the church. Until then, religion is nothing more than ego and judgment disguised as sincerity and false humility. The principle that I'm about to share with you, I share it not from the perspective of religious creed but, rather, from the perspective of revelation and personal experience, because I see it working within my own life and I know it to be true. "No" does not exist within the Kingdom of

Heaven. There is only unlimited Oneness without division, complete and total agreement, and perfectly balanced "Divine Union." The Father, the Son, and the Holy Spirit aren't constantly at war with each other, with each attempting to assert authority, one over the other. No. Absolutely not. The Godhead – the Source – is not schizophrenic or bipolar. The Godhead does not exist with multiple personality disorder. There is one, singular will and one singular mind. That mind is the Divine Mind of the Holy Spirit. I share this with you to simply say that we, too, are a part of this Divine Union and this eternal Oneness. Within the Kingdom there is only "Yes." Allow me to explain this principle in this way, with a simple question: Does God get what He desires? The question itself might seem to be a misnomer of sorts, upon first thought. However, the way that you choose to answer this question will serve as a direct reflection of your own sensitivity to your own creative power – the awakening of the inner Kingdom of Heaven within you. The scriptures are replete with passages, detailing that all things exist within Him and that all things were made by Him, for the simple purpose of bringing pleasure to Himself. The creation – His matchless handiwork – was "good," in His sight. Now, though, more than two millennia since some of the early writings were first recorded, humanity, unfortunately, seems to have become anesthetized to the truth of its own creative power. A very popular song depicts the dichotomy in this way: "Some of God's greatest gifts are unanswered prayers." Well, although the song provides a lovely sentiment – that sometimes the greatest blessings comes from "unanswered prayers," what if I were to tell you that never even once has a prayer gone unanswered and that never once has God responded to your desire with a "No?" You would, perhaps, find that claim outlandish and shocking and, depending upon your own, ingrained religious lens, might even consider the statement to be blasphemous, even.

However, prophetically speaking, I know it to be the truth. You see, within the Kingdom there is no dichotomy whatsoever: there is only one singular stream of creative power. The dichotomy – the sense of "yes" and "no" is created from within our own selves, through our own programmed filters. As I discussed in great detail within my book *The Universe Is At Your Command*, the universe, quite literally, has no ulterior motive of its own, as it exists and radiates within complete and total and absolute order and balance and well-intention. There is only a stream of well-intention flowing – not two separate streams of "good" and "bad." How often have you and I been told the damnable and erroneous religious lie that seems to suggest it is God who is picking and choosing, selectively, who to bless and who to curse. My friend, that erroneous lie isn't even Biblical in any way whatsoever. Why is it so vitally important to have a vision board in our daily lives? Quite simply, because the Kingdom of Heaven doesn't respond to wishful, hope-filled prayers; the universe will only respond to harnessed and focused intention and strong faith. I want to share with you something that may come as quite a shock; however, if you can receive this truth by the Holy Spirit, never again will you ever be the same. "God has never said 'No' to you; you simply failed to harness your own intention." When I say this, please bear in mind that I'm referring specifically to the process of creational manifestation, as it relates to the power of attraction. I'm not seeking to suggest in any way that there isn't a natural order to things. Yes, there will be a point at which we will, all, die, and leave the body, bound for eternity with Jesus. However, when creating with our own focused intent, for the purposes of our own good pleasure, there is never "No," there is only "Yes." My friend, the universe has always given you what you wanted; based upon the intention – the signal – you were sending out with your thoughts. Therein lies the seemingly great paradox of existence. I often describe it in this way: "In order to see your life change, you must allow every fiber of your being to bend to the law of flexibility." In other words, take control of the things that you can control and, for all the rest, learn to have faith. However, when creating with your thoughts, make your demands boldly, knowing that the Kingdom is responding strictly to your own, harnessed will and intention. The Law of Attraction is operating at all times, and it is continuously reminding us that we are the creators of our own lives. When the Holy Spirit inspired me to write *Creating With Your Thoughts,* I felt a Divine, prophetic unction to discuss within it the very real and tangible distinction that exists between the spirit and the soul. Understanding this difference is not only crucial in beginning to understand the power of our thought forms, but the understanding reminds us also of the importance of utilizing a vision board. As I was writing the book, the Spirit encouraged me to view the spirit as the true Self and the soul as merely the vehicle – the filter – through which we experience the temporal world. It is for this reason that we must learn to become sensitive to the voice of the Holy Spirit, because so often the soul – the mind, the will, and our emotions – can be misleading, at times. It rarely ever possesses the full picture, as it is continuing to learn and to grow and to awaken. The Holy Spirit which Jesus gives, however, leads us into all truth. In discussing the mechanics behind a vision board, it is important to once again revisit this distinction between the soul and the spirit; however, I now feel led to share the difference in a more unique way: by discussing the mind and body correlation. This unique correlation which exists between the mind and the body helps us to see even more deeply into the hidden recesses of the creative power we are enacting when utilizing a vision board. According to James Allen, "A person is limited only by the thoughts that he chooses." I know this to be the case. I often like to say it in this way: "The system of this world is nothing more than man's own creation, birthed first within the mind of the heart." You see, literally everything that we see and experience daily within the physical world is merely an outward reflection – a sort of hologram, really – of the inner Kingdom, within, being manifested externally. As we've discussed previously, all matter, literally everything and every "thing" within the physical, world is made up and composed of a very metaphysical energy. This energy of creation responds solely to thought and to intention. Our desires – the visions upon our vision board – are fuel which triggers the inspiration to flow, which, in turn, brings forth the creation into the earth realm, tangibly for all to see. In other words, by creating according to our deepest and truest desire, we are bringing for the inner Kingdom of Heaven into the earth realm – making the Kingdom and the will of God come to earth, just as it is in Heaven. By creating, we are literally becoming the answer to the prayer Jesus prayed. Everything begins *within*, in the inner realm of the heart space – within the thought. However, with each passing thought and with each decree made, based upon our desires, there are literal interactions which take place between the inner realm and the physical, natural body. In other words, the inner Kingdom of Heaven is literally changing even the energies of our human bodies. This is why miraculous healings are able to take place and why accounts of supernatural healing were so rampant throughout the early church, as documented throughout the book of Acts. The Apostle Paul speaks of the mind and body correlation numerous times throughout his epistles to the early churches. Throughout his epistles he often speaks of transformation – literal metamorphosis – from one plane of existence to another plane of existence. He depicts a constant state of merging between two worlds – Heaven and Earth and Soul and Body. In his mystical writings, detailed in Romans 12:2, he described the transformation in this way: "And be not conformed to this world: but be ye *transformed* by the renewing of your *mind*, that ye may prove what *is* that good, and acceptable, and perfect, will of God." The transformation of all things begins within the mind, as the inner will of the Godhead is reflected outwardly for all to see. The inner vision transforms us – spirit, soul, and body. This transformation is described perfectly, again and in a telling way, in Philippians 3:20-21, in a passage in which the Apostle Paul speaks of a literal physical transformation. In the original writing, within the context of resurrection, he uses the Greek term "soma," rather than "pneuma" to depict a transformation within the literal, physical human body. Prior to this passage, in Philippians 3:11, Paul writes of his ambition of hoping to attain the resurrection; however, the term used in the original writing is "ek anastasis," which, in Greek, means "out-resurrection." When viewed within the context of his other epistles regarding transformation, it becomes quite clear that Paul stressed the importance of continually being "brought to life" through the processes of *inner* transformation. When speaking of vision boards, it is important to remember that we are speaking of a tool which will aid us in our attempt to merge, or blend, two worlds – the inner world and the outer, physical world – in order to bring an inner vision into the earth realm to be enjoyed and experienced and touched, bodily and tangibly. A vision board reminds us that we can come to life again and again and again, over and over, and can continually create and recreate our lives according to our own will – our will being the very will of the Godhead. Far too often, when a feeling of hopelessness arises, we begin to feel as though there will be no more life and no more adventure ahead. My friend, this is simply not the case. The inner Kingdom – Heaven within – will simply not allow that to happen! You and I will always continue to dream and desire and, as a result, will always cast vision for our lives and our futures. Today, I want you to be encouraged and inspired to remember that with each and every desire you are being reminded that brighter days are ahead. In fact, the very fact that you are continuing to desire and to envision future roads ahead and future experiences that you'd love to enjoy is proof that the journey isn't over just yet. I want to encourage you, my friend, to always remember that your dreams are indicators that your journey is just beginning and that, regardless of what life may have seemingly thrown in your direction, your desires are reminders that your story doesn't have to end this way. As I often say, "The next chapter of your life can – and should – be the very best chapter of your life."

TALES OF THE VISION BOARD

ೞ

Whenever you begin to even think about and ponder the future "You," what do you see? I love the song "Ten Years, by the brilliant and incomparable Paul Simon. In the lyrics, he asks, "If you look into your future life ten years from this question do you imagine a familiar light burning in the distance?" What a beautifully transcendent question, don't you think? However, how very true, also, if you think about it. Regardless of how very far we travel and regardless of the many dreams and visions we manifest, the memory will remain, serving as a reminder of just how very far we've traveled and of just how very much we've truly accomplished. As I look back upon thirty years of my work – well, even upon ten years – I find myself in state of awe. I feel such an immense sense of gratitude to the Creator and to the Spirit for allowing me the immense privilege of being able to not only enjoy my life and my work and to in some way have impacted the lives of individuals throughout the world; however, I also know, instinctually, that there is so much more. The thought of more often boggles the mind, doesn't it? I mean, after having enjoyed such success and such immense adventure, traveling the world with my work all these years – meeting wonderful people just like you – how could it possibly get any better? Well, the truth of the matter is that I'm still dreaming, still desiring, and still casting vision for my life and for those I love. The adventure never truly ends. If energy never ends and merely changes form, as science suggests, then there is so much more to be enjoyed in this life and even beyond.

Dreams never truly die. Vison never truly dies. However, as we move beyond, forward and onward into even greater dreams, I want to ask you a very simple question. What does the future "You" look like? I have a dear friend named John who, to me, has one of the most amazing and remarkable examples of a prophetic vision board being put into practice. A successful man who has already accomplished so much in his life up to this point, he will be the first to say to the world that a vision board was such a pivotal part of his transforming his life. He shared a story with me that I want to share with you. I want you to remember this unforgettable story as you begin to build your very own dream life and continue to cast your own visions for your own bright future. When he told me this story, it literally sent chills down my spine, because it's so bizarre and otherworldly. It's beautifully haunting, really. John had just recently moved into a new home. As you know, perhaps from your own experiences with moving from one location to another, moving can be quite a chore. There were boxes and boxes everywhere. He had just moved to a new city. One day, John looked over to see his young son sitting atop one of the boxes, amidst all the clutter of the move. The small boy asked, "Dad, what's in this box?" John explained to his son that the box contained just a few old items from the attic and opened the box to see. As he opened the box, he pulled from within it one of his very first vision boards he had ever created. It was old, but sturdy. Knowing, years before, that poster board will rarely ever last and can easily become torn, John made his first vision board upon a wooden tablet – a literal board – that would last for years. He explained to his young son that the object was his vision board and tried to explain to him – in terms he could understand – just how powerful it is to dream and to write those dreams down. As he wiped the dust away from the board, though, John noticed something that frightened him. The picture of the home that he had placed onto the board all those years and year prior – years before the children and years before the marriage, while he was living in another city – was the exact same home he had just moved into. No, it wasn't a similar home. Now, it wasn't a home that had many of the same qualities and an eerily similar exterior. It was the *exact* same house. The Kingdom had provided him with a dream that he had seemingly forgotten about. Heaven, however, had remembered the old contract. He shared with me, "Jeremy, years ago, I had absolutely no plan to move into this city. When I posted the picture I didn't even know where the home was located." It changed him. Understandably. It's so very easy, isn't it, to remind Heaven of the many promises made. However, how very often have we made note of all the promises kept? How often have we ever stopped to think of just how many times Heaven has already provided? Of just how often the dreams did come to pass? A vision board reminds us not only of our past dreams, but it reminds us of the many times that Heaven remembered the promise and kept its end of the bargain. For a moment, I'd like for you to image where you were ten years ago. Even if you were, then, in your current city or town. I'd like for you to think of your experiences, then, and now.

You're in no way the same person you were. Even if you're now living within the same home and still working the exact same job and have not created a new dream for yourself *yet*, you are in no way the same person you were. If you had any experience that you enjoyed – if you ever had the opportunity to love – you are changed in some way. Think of the friendships you made – the people who, seemingly, randomly, came into your life at the most unexpected times. Think of the times with family – the many, many memories made. Think of the times you laughed. Think of some of those devastating heartbreaks that you said you'd never survive. Yet, here you are – still moving forward. You're still dreaming. My friend, if you were to have written down upon a vision board, then, the dreams and the desires of your heart, just imagine how many of those dreams and desires you'd now be able to look back on today as having already come to pass. The vision board serves as a reminder to us, not only of our future, but also as a testament of how very far we've come. It reminds us of just how much we've grown – how much life we've truly experienced. Moments matter. This thing called "life" is but a series of moments. The Apostle Paul says it's like a "vapor," really. It changes and evolves – transforms – so, so very quickly. When I look back even upon the past five years of my life, I'm filled with immense gratitude and pride and an overwhelming sense of joy and thankfulness. I've made new friends. I've accomplished so much more than I would have ever dreamed twenty years ago. I held the hands of a few close loved ones as they've drawn their final breaths and returned home. I've seen and experienced so much. In fact, just within the past week, I've had the opportunity to coach new clients and make new friends. The journey and the adventure of life are constantly, constantly being created, over and over again, day by day. Today, I want to encourage you to begin to see the future "You" in a way that completely transcends the new home, the new, car, the new relationships, and the larger bank account. I want you, for a moment, to begin to see the many, many wonderful people, the places – the experiences – of your life. If you were to be completely honest with yourself, I dare say you'd count yourself pretty blessed to have been a part of some of those wonderful experiences, in spite of some of those painful moments. When the prophet of old, the prophet Habakkuk, was instructed to write the vision down and to make it plain, he was told that there would be a time at which the vision would begin to speak for him and that it would not lie. The same can be said of us. Your vision speaks for you from the board you create. It doesn't lie. It can't lie, because the vision was birthed from within the Divine Mind of the Holy Spirit. Your dreams have come from God, not from within your own heart. In fact, your heart is the very heartbeat of God – your desires His very own pulse. You and I are extensions of the Creator, endowed with the same powerful force which hurled the stars onto the canvas of the night sky and framed the worlds in the heavens above us. What a beautiful thing this thing we call "life." Each day I awaken to a new day, I'm filled with a sense of overwhelming optimism. It brings tears to my eyes, really, if I were to be completely honest with you. Your life, for all the good and regardless of all the seemingly not-so-good, has been a masterpiece of your own creation. Sure, sometimes the canvas has gotten a little messy, and it's looked a lot more, at times, like the brush strokes of a child rather than the brush strokes of a master painter – it's looked more abstract that at other times. However, even those seemingly messy moments were the product of a very Divine Mind. Even those messy moments serve as proof that you were learning and growing. The relationship that ended so abruptly and so unexpectedly, it served a purpose, really. It helped you learn to see what you are truly deserving of and what you truly want. The career that's seemingly been draining the life out of you, it's serving to help you realize that, yes, you really can do better for yourself. It's reminding you to see that, yes, you really can move forward and start something fresh. For all the good and for all the seemingly not-so-good, you've really been learning to create better – to become a more conscientious creator of your life. Trust me; I know it definitely didn't seem like it at the time. When I'm speaking to my clients in coaching sessions, I always want them to learn to recognize the greater good of all the experience of their lives. Awakening comes from being able to see the greater good of each and every leg of the journey, recognizing that it all happened for a reason. When we begin to utilize the vision board within our daily lives, we are reminded of the inner dreamer – we're awakened to that deeper dream. We find ourselves inspired and emboldened to keep going. Just as my good friend John found himself in amazement at just how perfectly the Kingdom answered his own dreams, so, too, can you and I be inspired to recognize that this same creative power is always at work within us, as well. Whenever you write down your vision upon your vision board and begin to make it plain for Heaven to see, keep in mind that regarding the powerful energies of creation beginning to be enacted the moment you place your pen to paper to create your board, the story is beginning to be written – a new and exciting chapter. Not even Hollywood could imagine the beauty of the life you begin to create the moment that you begin to take that very first step of faith. Even you will be surprised by the perfect precision of Heaven. You will find yourself literally in shock and awe at just how carefully choreographed and painstakingly, strategically maneuvered the forces of creation will begin to be. The move, the breakup, the night out with friends, the evening concert you enjoyed under the stars with your favorite person, it's all is part of the greater grander picture being created. It's all part of a building project – it's all construction being enacted. A beautiful work is being erected in a place where there was once only a vacant lot. A dream is beginning to emerge. My friend, I assure you, the moment that you begin to view your life in this way – not merely from the perspective of cause-and-effect and coincidental happenstance – but, rather from the full knowledge that you, yourself, are always, at all times, playing a very active role within the process of your own creation, everything will begin to emerge and manifest more quickly and effortlessly. All of the sudden, that creative power – that power that formed all that is – will begin to emerge before your very own eyes. You will see clearly and the eyes of your heart will become illuminated to the greater and grander truth that you and I have always been in perfect harmony and within perfect union with the Creator. Remove even the notion of coincidence from your mind and vocabulary. There are no coincidences – no happenstance. The universe is far too meticulous for things such as that. It's all part of the great design of the Divine Mind, and you and I could not possibly be any more connected and one with that Divine Mind than we already are. Nothing can separate us from the beautiful and perfect love that is always inspiring us. When I think of the mind-baffling concept of eternal Oneness – our union with the Creator – I am reminded of the words of the psalmist and of the words of the Apostle. "Whither shall I go from thy spirit? Or whither shall I flee from thy presence? If I ascend up into heaven, thou art there: if I make my bed in hell, behold thou art there. If I take the wings of the morning, and dwell in the uttermost parts of the sea; even there shall thy hand lead me, and thy right hand shall hold me." (Psalm 139:7-10) "For I am persuaded that neither death, nor life, nor angels, nor principalities, nor powers, nor things present, nor things to come, nor height, nor depth, nor any other creature, shall be able to separate us from the love of God, which is in Christ Jesus our Lord." (Romans 8:38-39) Try as we may, there is no escaping the power of

208

creation. There is no escaping the love which surrounds us at all times, continually. Only one word comes to mind to describe the power of creation: "forever."

THE INNER SIGHT

ೞ⧓

"If I can visualize it, then I know I can do it! If God has allowed us to think it, then He has empowered us to do it!" – Jeremy Lopez

Everything that we see with our natural eyes emerges from a world that cannot be seen with natural sight. This is, in essence, the true heart of the vision board at work. Far, far too often, we allow ourselves to become so anesthetized to the inner world – the inner voice and the inner sight – that we allow ourselves to begin to feel completely and utterly dependent upon the natural world alone. This is simply not the case. Always, at all times, there is an inner vision being enacted within us, and if we can simply learn to take the time to begin to look within – from the internal perspective – then we will change the outward manifestation and, too, the outward movement of our daily life. Deepak Chopra, the brilliant mind behind many spiritual teachings, described the mechanics of a vision board in this way, per the writings of the Chopra Center: "You know how when you get a new car, you see that particular make and model everywhere you go? That's because you have put your attention on something specific, and are unconsciously scanning the world for items that match it. It's not that those cars were never there; it's simply that you never noticed them before." This principle describes perfectly the process of visualization within our own lives. This example, and its truth, is proof-positive that we are always, whether we realize it consciously or not, looking at the world from an internal set of eyes – the eyes of the Soul. Truly, as I've described in detail so many times before, you and I are the "observer" of our own creative processes. We're always looking outward onto the plane of the physical world and, in very real and literal ways, acting upon it from our own unique perspectives. Picture the process in this way. As I've shared before, two people can take the same exact trip to the same exact destination and, upon returning home, recall the trips completely differently. Why? Because, through inner vision, we are each interpreting the world around us – the natural, outward world – from our own unique perspectives of our own, inner sight. You've, I'm sure, heard it said before that seeing is believing? Well, it's true. Life lived from the perspective of the natural and the physical says, "I have to see it in order to believe it." However, life lived from the place of vision and the inner dream boldly declares, "If I can believe it then I can see it." The illustration described by Dr. Chopra – suddenly seeing your new car everywhere – well, Dr. John Assaraf terms the process "neural reconditioning." Whether you realize it or not, your vision board is literally rewiring – literally reconditioning – your brain. As we've discussed previously, when we set the vision before our eyes, new neural pathways are being formed within the brain. These new neural pathways, due to the wonderful, biological truth of neural plasticity, are promoting and encouraging the furtherance of the desire to attain and the inspiration to become. My friend, through the utilization of the vision board, you and I are actually becoming our vision and beginning to walk out our dreams in the human plane of existence. This is more than mere metaphysical energy; this is science and biology. What an amazing thought to ponder that the Creator, in His infinite intelligence, created us to literally be able to manifest our dreams and desires by actually learning to focus upon them. What an incredible and transcendent power of creation you and I possess. As I share with my clients, literally on a daily basis, "What you think, you become." It's true. Megan Patiry, from the Academy of

Art University, in her article written for Huffington Post, says of her vision board, "Each morning, my career waves to me from my study wall. I'm talking about being greeted by my vision board." The vision board is a reminder to us of the power of the inner sight we possess. It reminds us, daily, of the tremendous power of our dreams by constantly aiding us in our focus – bringing our focus from the outward, temporal world, back into a sharp, laser-beam focus upon the inner vision. Jack Nicklaus, considered to be one of the greatest golfers of all times, has been quoted as saying, "I never hit a shot, not even in practice, without having a very sharp, in-focus, picture of it in my head." Well, just as champion athletes use the power of vision and inner sight to perfect their scores, so, too, can you and I harness the power of the inner sight to "see" our future lives, long before they ever begin to unfold. I'm often asked, "Is it the seeing or the believing that's most important?" Well, the truth of the matter is that it's both. The seeing and the believing are forever linked, interchangeably; there's really no difference between the two when we begin to access the world of the inner sight – the realm behind the vision depicted upon the vision board. In truth, you and I have always been walking vision board. From each thought and with each desire, we are constantly creating and triggering the powerful and forceful energies of the Creator in our daily lives. The universe, in its grand design, has always been highly subject to these energies and signals. Not even once have you and I been without vision. Many people are shocked to know that most heads of Fortune 500 companies implement vision boards into their work literally every day. I was coaching the head of a brokerage firm once, a man who spends his days leveraging asset on the exchange, and he exclaimed to me, "Before my team ever even hits the trading floor each morning, we have a thirty minute meeting going over our vision boards for the week. Since we've implemented vision boards, we've seen not only an increase in wealth but it's like the stress has been greatly diminished also. Now it's just fun!" When I often speak of "effortless manifestation," this is what I'm referring to, my friend. I'm in no way seeking to suggest that there is no literal work involved on our part, as creators. Of course, there is the aspect of personal responsibility being in play at all times. We have to position ourselves in such a way that we're able to receive the abundance when it comes. That means you can't simply sit on the couch all day long, watching television and expect the universe to give you your desires. It doesn't work that way. Continue to take responsibility in your daily life. If you have a job, continue to go, until you feel the inspiration for a new direction. If you have bills, continue to pay them. The process of creation isn't an excuse to no longer do your part. You and I must always continue to do our part, by being positioned in a way to receive. However, by utilizing a vision board, the process of manifestation begins to seem "effortless." I've heard these testimonies for as long as I can remember, since starting to teach my clients the importance of vision boards. Day after day, it seems, individuals, just like you, report to me the following testimony: "Everything began to take on more of a sense of fun." When you and I begin to see through the lens of the inner sight

– the inner eye, if you will – we begin to recognize that each day is a literal creative adventure. When you begin to see through the lens of your inner vision, gone will be the days of constant struggle and constant lack. My friend, although there are very real stressful moments that will always be a part of the human experience, please believe me when I say to you that life was never meant to be a time of constant struggle, where every day is a constant drain. That's not the abundant life Jesus spoke of. So, when I speak of the "inner sight," what am I speaking of? I'm referring to the change of perspective needed to propel the force of creation. The vision board will aid in this.

However, I want you to begin to develop such an immense sensitivity to the inner voice and to the inner sight that you will begin to awaken each day to world viewed through a new set of eyes – inner, spiritual eyes of hope. The "inner sight" I speak of is the lens of hope and the lens of the abundant life. It's the sight which says, "I can be a blessing to others." However, in order to be a blessing to others, you must first be blessed. This goes far, far beyond natural wealth, although it does take money to prosper in the natural world. My sincere hope and prayer for you, my friend, is that you will begin to live life each day from the place of the inner sight – through spiritual eyes of inspiration. See yourself as already having the new home or the new career or the new relationship. See your life as already filled with more joy and more peace and more prosperity and abundance, and, just as the scriptures of old teach us, "You will have what you say." Jesus described the process of creation in this way: "Therefore I say unto you, what things soever ye desire, when ye pray, believe that ye receive them and ye shall have them." (Mark 11:24) There is so much more to be said of this particular passage of scripture; however, when speaking of living life through the lens of the "inner sight," this passage describes the mechanics of creation perfectly. This far surpasses mere wishful thinking and a simple state of hopefulness or positivity. No, this goes far, far beyond mere emotion. Belief, within the context of this scripture is much, much more concrete and more tangible. The belief, described in the teachings of Jesus, speaks more of a solid and definitive form – containing mass and substance. Knowing this, the definition of faith described within the book of Hebrews begins to take on an entirely new and different meaning, does it not? That faith is the "substance?" So often, within my own life and within my own processes of visualization, I find my inner voice – the voice of the Spirit – constantly reminding me of the promises of my own dreams. The inner voice screams to me, daily, "Remember, Jeremy, you can have whatever you can see." From the very beginning, as the Spirit first moved and brooded upon the face of the deep, long before God ever uttered the words "Let there be light," there was an inner sight – an inner vision – within the force of the Divine Mind. The Creator envisioned the soon-coming masterpiece, long before He ever even uttered a word. Imagine that. The worlds were framed by the very real vision of the Godhead. Would the Godhead create flippantly or haphazardly, simply throwing out decrees and commands without ever really giving them thought? Of course not. What an absurd concept. There was focused intent and a sharply-attuned, finely-focused will and thought as the Creator uttered those words. Within the inner eye of the Divine Mind, there was already an image in place of what the desired intended result would look like. Just as the scriptures teach that the heavens were framed by the very word of God, it could just as correctly and rightly be said that the worlds were formed by the very thought – the inner vision of God. When uttering those words, "Let there be light," the Creator was simply giving utterance to the internal image already existing within His own heart. With that powerful force of creation, He watched as His words became a reality. He called it "good." Today, like all days, you are being given a choice. You may not have realized it yet, but there has always been the choice. The choice before you is the issue of perspective. It's the issue of sight. The universe, always, at all times, has been lovingly attempting to encourage you and ask, "Which eyes are you using to view your life?" The external eyes of natural sight, or the inner eyes – the inner sight – of the inner vision? Everything will rise and fall entirely upon your perspective of your own sight. If you can see it, then you can absolutely have it. If you can see it, then you will absolutely possess it. The issue, my friend, isn't merely a question of "what" you are seeing. The far more important question is, in fact, the issue of "how" you are seeing it. Everything is contingent upon the focus and the intent – which eyes are being used to determine the intended outcome and the expected end. I promise you, the expected end result of your life is "good." Can you see it yet?

THE ABUNDANT LIFE

CRANO

The moment that the intention was set and the harnessed, focused will was garnered, the words were spoken: "Let there be." In an instant, everything changed. Nothing would ever be the same again. Gone was the apparent darkness which seemed to, like a heavy blanket, cover the cosmos. There was, instead, a blinding light. Creation, though, did not end there. The Creator, for the purposes of His own good pleasure, continued to create, as all creators do. Feeling an inner desire for even more, He framed the many worlds, both within our galaxy and beyond. He created rivers and lakes and streams. He separated from the water dry land and made it inhabitable. However, the Creator did not stop there. He continued to create what would be His own crowning achievement. He created, then, a creation that would serve as the hallmark of His own will and His own intent. He crafted a creation so deeply personal and so connected to His own heart that

He even, before creating, said that the work would be in His very own image. With that, He reached down and with his own hand formed a man. The tale of Creation, described within the ancient scriptures, details it this way: "And God said, Let us make man in our image, after our likeness: and let them have dominion over the fish of the sea, and over the fowl of the air, and over the cattle, and over all the earth, and over every creeping thing that creepeth upon the earth. So God created man in his own image, in the image of God created he him; male and female created he them. And God blessed them, and God said unto them, Be fruitful, and multiple, and replenish the earth, and subdue it:

and have dominion over the fish of the sea, and over the fowl of the air, and over every living thing that moveth upon the earth." (Genesis 1:26-28) Then, with one taste of the so-called forbidden fruit, man developed the "knowledge of good and evil," according to the story and began to *feel* so very disconnected from the Creator. Then religion came. For centuries man, feeling so very disconnected within his mind, attempted to please God once again. Then Jesus came. Thankfully. He helped to awaken the consciousness of man to cause him to realize that there had always been absolute union and that, regardless of feeling disconnected, there is only Oneness within the

Godhead and Oneness connecting all things. Today, though, there are still so very many who have been so very anesthetized by the powerful drug of religion. In turn, they have convinced themselves that they are in no way deserving of the abundant life promised them. Rather than walking in their fullness, they, instead, say things like, "I'm *just* a sinner saved by grace." "If it's God's will, I'll be better." "If the Lord wants me to have more, He'll give it to me." Or, better yet, "Why does God bless others and not me?" The vicious cycle continues to this day, as day in and day out, much of humanity continues to remain blinded within their mind to the truth of the creative power. My friend, not

235

only is abundance and wealth your God-given birthright, it is your inheritance. Wealth in no way refers only to material things and to worldly possessions; however, make no mistake. It does include it. Over the years, I've heard so many people ask, "Jeremy, are you one of those prosperity preachers?" Well, let me say that I'm definitely not a poverty preacher. My friend, I believe, wholeheartedly, in the abundant life which Jesus promised. I live it and experience it daily. I say that not to be proud or boastful, but I say that, rather, to encourage you to begin seeing yourself as the literal extensions of the Creator within the earth realm. For me, the moment I became fully awakened to the great and vast truth of creative power – The Law of Creation – gone were the days of simply sitting idly by, allowing life to pass me by. No, instead I began to use my God-given potential to begin to attract into my life all that I desire. I began to create according to the patterns and the purposes that the Spirit had birthed within my heart. In order to amass great wealth and a worldly fortune? No. In order to be a blessing to the world and to those around me, so that others would see the goodness of God and the vast wealth of the universe. That being said, however, I realized years and years ago that the moment we begin to purpose in our hearts that we are the creators of our lives, according to the promise of God within the earth realm, I realized, in an instant, that literal abundance and prosperity were beginning to track me down and follow me wherever I went. I began to see my vision – the inner desires of my heart – come to life like never before. Today, I now live the dreams that I once dreamed years ago. Each day, now, I awaken to a life in which I get to experience and enjoy the fruits of my labor and the blessings which I have attracted into my own, personal life. The dreams and the visions, for me, became a reality. Still, I dream new dreams and the dreams continue to come – along with the manifestations. You see, the power of creation never ceases to flow. Creation never ends, because of The Law of Creation and The Law of Attraction being enacted through the powerful minds we've been entrusted with. I refuse to settle. I refuse to live within lack. Did you know that the scriptures teach that money answers everything? Study the scriptures. I promise you that you will find exponentially more passages of scripture concerning wealth and prosperity than you ever will poverty and lack. Lack stems from the mentality of disconnectedness – the feeling of being so separate from others and from the resources of God. I share much more on this topic in my course, *The School of Visualization*, particularly the lesson entitled, *Connecting to Creation Resources*. My friend, for a moment I'd like for you to allow one simple truth to awaken your heart. I pray that you receive this powerful truth: "I am here to experience an abundant life." Allow that truth to sink deeply into your heart and mind and to permeate your very essence. I've often said before that God truly doesn't care if you drive a Honda or a Toyota or a Mercedes or a Bentley. It doesn't matter to Him. Why? Because it's your heart that matters. For centuries and centuries, humanity has allowed itself to fall victim to the bondage of religion – always looking upon the outward. Have you ever stopped to think that maybe part of the reason you don't have what you truly desire if because for most of your life you've looked to those who do have great wealth and drive the nice car and have judged them in your heart? You cannot judge the very thing you desire to have. By doing so, you disconnect yourself from the flow of inspiration which is the fuel of creation. You become double-minded, rather than driven forward by focused, harnessed intent, and the scriptures teach us that a double-minded person is unstable in all their ways. It doesn't matter to God if you work in an office, in a cubicle, or if you are the head of the Fortune 500 Company. You get to decide. You get to choose the life that you get to experience, because you, being driven the power of the Spirit – the voice of the inner Kingdom – are the creator of your own, earthly experiences. For me, I chose long ago to enjoy the abundant life. For me, I refuse to go back. Show me someone who judges the wealth of another man and I will show you someone who lives in poverty. My friend, it's a universal principle – a principle of the Kingdom of Heaven. Like will always attract like. You have what you say, and you become what you think and what you have purposed within your heart. You and I were meant to be a blessing to others, within the earth realm. In order to do that, you and I must be blessed. You're probably now understanding why I began this book by encouraging you to begin to see yourself as deserving of having your desire fulfilled. In order to experience the abundant life promised us, you and I must begin to see ourselves as being completely at one with the Creator. In truth, there is no distinction of wills and no distinction of desires. Your will is the will of the Creator, made manifest within the earth realm. Your desires are His desires. Each morning when I awaken to a brand new day, I see myself as the literal living and breathing extension of the Creator within this earth, and I encourage you to begin to see yourself in the exact same light. Only when you begin to see yourself as being deserving of having your desire fulfilled, will you truly surrender to the power of your own, creative force. So often, when thinking of the concepts of abundance and wealth and prosperity, the mind goes, solely, to the visionary images of money and materialism. My friend, this simply is not the case. Prosperity, wealth, and abundance are concepts that far, far supersede the materialistic aspects of reality. Sure, it takes money to make it in the world, but what about more joy? What about more of a peace of mind and more of a sense of contentment and a greater sense of intuition? There's so much more. What if I were to ask you when was the last time you actually remember having an inner sense of peace and a strong peace of mind? Has it been a while? For that matter, when was the last time that you actually felt good about your life and all that's in it? Has that been even longer? You see, abundance goes far beyond the natural world and touches upon the deepest and most innate emotions and feelings of creation. Wouldn't you like more of it all? More of the peace and more of the contentment? The moment that we begin to place our visions upon the vision board – the moment we sing the contract with the universe – we begin to place ourselves in a position to receive. Imagine, for a moment, the vision board being the ultimate sign of surrender to the voice of your own, inner soul. What would you like to manifest? What dreams do you want to begin to finally see in the coming days? The coming weeks? What do you want your life to look like in the next six months? How about the next year? The vision board triggers the awakening of the inner desire and causes us to become more prone to accepting the abundant life. My friend, if you cannot see it, you cannot have it; but you will also never have it if you feel underserving of it. I so often counsel clients in life coaching sessions who say, "Jeremy, I feel like I'm under a generational curse." So often, they share how, for generations, there always seemed to be a sense of lack plaguing the entire family. "My mother never had much. Her mother didn't either. Now, it's falling on me." The curse is very, very real, my friend. However, the curse of which I speak is not the work of some demonic force seeking to plague your life. No. The curse is the mind that has yet to awaken and become illuminated to the greater promises of prosperity and the abundant life. The true curse is the mind that continues to live within the old paradigms of confinement, feeling so disconnected and undeserving of the creative power it fully and truly possesses. Today, my heartfelt and humble prayer for you is that you would begin to awaken – not only in heart and in spirit but also in your own, emotional understanding of your very own life's path. Today, you are being given a choice. You are being asked, "Will you allow this new life to flourish?" Heaven, with a tender voice of love, is asking, "Are you truly ready for a new and much more abundant life?" If so, the only hindrance is your own lack of belief and acceptance.

THE SOUL KNOWS THE WAY

CRSRD

As we began this journey in to the power behind the vison board – you and I – I shared with you that just down the road from me there is now a building under construction. That, where there was once only an empty, vacant lot, there was the emerging steel skeleton of what is to be high-rise luxury condos. Well, even as of the time of this writing now, so much more work has been accomplished. The project has begun to take even more shape. Now, as I drive past the construction site, I can now see the individual rooms, now completely framed. There are windows now in place. The walls are up. The entranceways are now completely finished. I wonder what the architect must feel when he sees the construction site each day? I imagine the great sense of pride and accomplishment that must overwhelm him as he sees his vision being brought forth into the world. For him, what began as an inner vision is now quickly becoming a very real reality. Soon, the project will be complete and the condos will be sold. Within a matter of months, where there was once only an empty and barren lot, there will be life. There will be the sounds of the city and the sights of evenings enjoyed upon balconies overlooking the Magic City. And to think, it all began with a vision. So it is with us – you and I. As creators, having within us the capacity to envision and to dream and, then, to create, you and I have been entrusted with immense and immeasurable power – the very same power that formed the worlds in the galaxies. Through the Law of Attraction and The Law of Creation, you and I are, daily, being given a chance to determine the outcome of our lives. Now, having awakened to the greater and more miraculous truths of the universe and the creative forces of the Divine Mind, gone are the days when we felt so very disconnected and so isolated from the creation and from the Creator. Now, rather, we begin to see that we are willing and mindful creators, always working in partnership with Heaven. Nothing has ever been left to chance. Nothing at all has ever been the product of mere happenstance or coincidental action. There are no coincidences. There never have been. The life that you and I awaken to each and every morning with the rising of the sun is the life of creation. You awaken to a world that you have created, just as I do. I know, full well, that the idea of accepting personal responsibility can be quite an uncomfortable feeling, at first. It stings the pride and wounds the ego, at first, to recognize that there is no one else to blame – when the crutches are removed. It hurts at first, for a moment, to see that we, ourselves, have been responsible for the creation of our lives, through our own thoughts, our own words, and our own actions. Then, though, the inspiration begins to flow. The encouragement comes. The vision begins to be birthed. When awakening comes, you and I are given the moment of recognition at which we can begin to see that, in spite of all the pain and in spite of all the work left to be done, we can begin to build again. In fact, we can rebuild. We can create and craft new dreams for our own bright futures. In creating, we are limited only by what we think and by what we see. If you can see it, then you can most assuredly have it. If you can see it, then it can be yours. For more than thirty years, I've recognized this truth, firsthand, within my own, personal, daily life. Now, I enjoy the life that was once only the inner vision within my mind's eye, all those years ago. The future that I once dreamed for myself is now the daily reality that I experience. The same can be said for you. That you, too, have the power of creation flowing throughout your entire being and the limited abundance of all that is now flowing ever-so freely throughout the entirety of your very own life. There are, even now, great and vast wells of limitless, pure potentiality that have yet to be tapped. There is a vision – a blueprint – that has yet to be drafted. However, the moment that you and I begin to place pen to paper and craft a vision board for our own futures, something truly miraculous and otherworldly begins to happen. The power of creation begins to emerge into the physical, three-dimensional world of flesh and bone. By drafting the blueprint of the life we intend to construct, the miraculous begins to happen all around us. The entire universe begins to bend to our beckoned call. As I've said so many times before, truly, the universe is, indeed, at our command. *This* is what creators do. *This* is how creation operates. There is a reason that I have chosen to entitle this book to you *Creating Your Soul Map*, and I've decided to save that reason for the very last: your vision board is your external compass. It's the outward projection onto physical space and time the inner, metaphysical world of your dreams and desires. Your vision board is the visual tool of creation by which you and I and so, so many millions of other dreamers throughout the world begin to see and recognize daily that we are the architects of our own life creation. The Creator has entrusted us with His own powerful force of intention. Intention, as it were, has been hardwired into us, into the most innate fabric of our being. I want to share with you one last piece of scientific truth, in our discussion on the power behind the vision board, because I feel that, this piece of pertinent information will help you to see, full well, the power that you truly possess at all times. Together, you and I have taken a journey, together, into the deeper recesses of the human mind, the miraculous world of the Spirit, and into the deepest truths of human thought and behavior. However, at the very end, a vision board works because of a very scientific principle. I'm so often asked, "What is the secret behind 'the secret?'" Well, in truth, it's simple science and biology. The ascending reticular activating system, also known, simply as the ARAS, is a set of nuclei within the human brain that's responsible for regulating wakefulness and the transition into the dream state. Quite simply put, what science calls this "extra thalamic control modulatory system" is just the inner gauge of the brain which causes us to separate the dream state from the state of daily waking function. This is also the inner modulator and regulator which causes our eyes to gravitate toward the things that we desire. Scientifically and biologically speaking, this is the real reason why when you purchase a new car, all of the sudden you begin to see the same, exact car everywhere you turn, seemingly. It's because your consciousness – your inner perspective – has shifted and you now are able to see your own desires outwardly, manifested upon the outer, physical world. My friend, there is even now – right now in this very moment – a very real internal compass within you which is leading you toward your desires and toward your truest and deepest passions. I share this scientific truth with you to simply say, your soul has always known the way. Whether you realize it, consciously, or not, every movement and every thought has inadvertently been driving you forward all along, the entire time, toward a greater understanding of what it is that you truly want and desire. Your entire life, already, has been collecting data and information by which you can now, in this NOW moment, begin to see the life you truly have always dreamed. Your soul has always known the way, even when it didn't seem like it. What a magnificent life, this life of creation. My friend, it was always meant to be enjoyed and experienced and lived to the fullest. The abundant life is, indeed, the life of creation – a life lived through the lens of the inner vision and the inner dream. As you draft your vision, upon your own vision board, whether it be upon poster board or upon tablets of wood or even upon notebook paper or even upon stone tablets – however you choose – you are literally making a choice to become a conscientious and proactive, willing participant within the creation of your own life, rather than just a mere spectator, looking on from the sidelines. I can speak only for myself, when I say, I never again will sit on the sidelines of existence, looking on, watching my life pass me by. Creation is far too grand for that. The universe is far too methodical for that. The love of the Creator is far too immense for that. Truly, there is far, far too much life to be lived. I, for one, choose to enjoy it. If you've followed my work and my teachings from the very beginning of my own journey or if you've just seemingly happened upon this work because of your own curiosity about the power behind the vision board, my prayer for you, my dear friend, is that you would begin to finally live. Stop watching life pass you by. Take ownership of your own creative process. Take stock within the value of your life experiences. Finally, for the first time ever, begin to live out the life of your dreams.

ABOUT THE AUTHOR

Dr. Jeremy Lopez is Founder and President of Identity Network and Now Is Your Moment. Identity Network is one of the world's largest prophetic resource sites and distributes books, eBooks, and teachings to a global audience. Dr. Lopez is an international, highly-sought dream coach, teacher, and philosopher who for more than thirty years has served as a leading voice within the prophetic movement and has counseled audiences throughout the world to unlock their hidden, untapped potential. He is the bestselling author of more than thirty books, including *The Universe Is At Your Command* and *Creating With Your Thoughts*. He is considered by many to be one of the world's foremost leading experts on the topic of The Law of Attraction and has personally served as advisor to heads of business and heads of state. He has delivered prophetic insight to Governor Bob Riley of Alabama and also to Israeli Prime Minister Benjamin Netanyahu. The teachings of Dr. Lopez are being utilized around the world in various conferences and training centers, and many dreamers are becoming awakened because of his great understanding of the mysteries, cycles, and patterns of the universe. Dr. Lopez continues to write, travel, and teach extensively.

ADDITIONAL WORKS

The Universe Is At Your Command:
Vibrating the Creative Side of GOD

Creating With Your Thoughts

Prophetic Transformation

Abandoned To Divine Destiny

Awakening to Prosperity

The Law of Attraction: Universal Power
of Spirit

And many more

53450584R00173

Made in the USA
San Bernardino, CA
15 September 2019